T0194584

An Inside Look at
EDUCATION

What No One Told Us and How It Is Impacting Our Children

Sylvia McCrory

WESTBOW
PRESS®
A DIVISION OF THOMAS NELSON
& ZONDERVAN

WestBow Press books may be ordered through booksellers or by contacting:

WestBow Press
A Division of Thomas Nelson & Zondervan
1663 Liberty Drive
Bloomington, IN 47403
www.westbowpress.com
844-714-3454

ISBN: 978-1-6642-4397-2 (sc)
ISBN: 978-1-6642-4398-9 (hc)
ISBN: 978-1-6642-4396-5 (e)

Library of Congress Control Number: 2021918016

Print information available on the last page.

WestBow Press rev. date: 09/14/2021

This book is dedicated to all parents who are interested in or struggling with rearing their children with Christian values and a firm foundation. We empathize and wish we could have had access to a series of books like this when rearing our children. Though it may seem that we are displaying a lot of negative information about each topic, we are presenting the most current information available to us at this time. Please read with a Christian heart, looking for the evils of the world from which to protect children.

CONTENTS

GOD HAS DIRECTED US, AS PARENTS, TO INSTRUCT OUR CHILDREN

Imprint these words of mine on your hearts and minds, bind them as a sign on your hands, and let them be a symbol on your foreheads. Teach them to your children, talking about them when you sit in your house and when you walk along the road when you lie down and when you get up. (Deuteronomy 11:18–19 CSB)

Command those who are rich in this present world not to be arrogant nor to put their hope in wealth, which is so uncertain, but to put their hope in God, who richly provides us with everything for our enjoyment. Command them to do good, to be rich in good deeds, and to be generous and willing to share. In this way, they will lay up treasure for themselves as a firm foundation for the coming age, so that they may take hold of the life that is truly life. (1 Timothy 6:17–19 NIV)

Throughout the ages, parents have given their children over to educators to train and educate. In many cases, parents were not educated; some could not read or write. There are still some illiterate parents today, or parents unable to understand English. Schools, tutors, and mentors are wonderful for students to gain knowledge. In general, educators have expertise in specific subjects and have spent years learning and studying to become proficient and knowledgeable. With this much training and studying, it makes sense to want our children to gain some of this valuable knowledge.

At church, we are happy to drop our children off at their Sunday school class or Bible study class. They gain so much knowledge from these wonderful people of God. Our children also love to see their friends and attend all the great activities. To be honest, very few of us put much time and effort into preparing our children for church. We spend much more time preparing them for school. This is where we continue to get it wrong: we are preparing them for worldly life, not a heavenly life.

These wonderful people at school and church are educators for our children, and they add a great deal of insight and instruction. However, they are not given the complete authority of instructing our children. The Bible tells parents that we are to instruct our children. The other educators are in addition to the instruction we are to give them. We should be overseeing our children's education and adding to it. We should be equipping them to face the world, which has moved away from Christian values. And we should constantly be looking at ourselves to see whether we are living up to the Christian values we are teaching.

Take time each day to pray that we are showing the love of God through our lives. Pray that our children are seeing God and His love in us. We should pray for our children every day by name. We should take the time to raise them before the throne of God and proclaim them to Him. Pray for their salvation, that they will be an instrument used to glorify God. Thank God for giving them to us to raise, but acknowledge that they belong to God. Thank God for the joys and blessings He has bestowed upon our families.

As you go through the study, keep in mind that Sylvia and Melissa have combined experience in the field of education totaling almost forty years. Sylvia researches and writes about the concerns and challenges parents face today. Melissa serves as advisor and collaborator, using her experience as an educator, parent and grandparent. They have taught in multiple grade levels that encompass private preschool, public school kindergarten through eighth grade, and community college. They have held positions as department chairs, specialists, and mentors. In addition, their experiences go beyond the classroom and include being on various decision and policy-making committees and creating planning guides and schedules for their schools, grade levels, and classrooms. Much of the content of this chapter reflects not only research but also personal experiences and insight into the changes impacting students and the proposed path of education.

They have observed the evolution of education and the changes in the philosophy of education. They have seen the gradual change in teaching moving away from being student centered to being data and technology centered. At the same time, they have seen the family dynamic change with extremes of parenting styles, from those who display little interest in their children to parents who are helicopter and lawnmower parents. The needs of children have given way to the needs of administrators, parents, and lawmakers to show concrete data.

We have reached an age where everyone wants to compare children against each other. No longer are children allowed to be children without some form of yardstick to measure their every move. Praise is wonderful for children. However, praise does not need to be delivered with a piece of paper or a trophy. Children should be afforded the comfort of being themselves, good or bad. Even when children fail, they need to know you still love them and are proud of them.

I fear that parents are conditioning children to believe the piece of paper or the trophy is the token they need to be loved. Many children feel when they fail, they will disappoint their parents and lose their love. I encourage parents to constantly kiss, hug, cuddle, and say "I love you" to their children. Please refrain from displaying your love on social media. Social media is not reassuring children—it is only fulfilling something for parents.

It is our hope and prayer that parents will gain a deeper, fuller love for God in this study. We also hope you will find Christian roots and foundations to establish within your family in order to rear your children as Christians. If you are not a Christian, or if your children are not, it is our prayer that we will bring comfort, support, and love to lead these precious children into the fold of God. It is also our intent to alert parents to the dangers and evils in our world so parents may be more informed and equipped to protect their children as they grow.

This information is presented to Christians but written to all parents from the hearts of two servants of God. Please, if you have not come to know the Lord Jesus Christ as your personal Savior, contact us or your local Christian minister. It is our prayer to protect children and bring others into the family of God.

With much love and thanks,
Sylvia McCrory
Melissa Wingfield

> Lord,
> I know You are with me and love me. Give me peace of mind as I prepare for this time of study. Give me insight that I might understand what I am studying, and help me to remember it when the time comes.
> In Jesus Name, Amen.

CHAPTER 1

Why American Students Are Tested so Much

The fear of the Lord is the beginning of wisdom, and knowledge of the Holy One is understanding. (Proverbs 9:10 NIV)

Americans today are on a quest for independence, wealth, power, fame, and abundance—that fast-paced, instant-gratification push to the head of the line. Cheating if necessary has become the present narrative. Long gone are the days of contentment and humbleness. Greed and control are the driving forces in this climate.

This may sound callous, especially if the description is of ourselves and our families. But if we are describing others, most would agree it is an accurate depiction of Americans.

Before we delve deeper into this subject, let us be clear that this did not happen overnight. Parents and educators are doing what they genuinely believe is the best for their children. Parents and teachers are investing a lot of time and money into improving test scores and reading levels. Our society and culture have been told repeatedly that the only road to success for our children is to obtain higher test scores. Now, in theory this sounds reasonable and logical. In fact, I was once an educator with the same ideals and beliefs.

The theory is if children are all tested by the same standards, they will all have the same knowledge, and teachers will be forced to teach the same curriculum. In short, teachers will be expected to cover the same material, and children will have exposure to the same information with no regard given to where they live or their socioeconomic situations. One of the most important arguments was that any students transferring during the school year would not be behind. All students will be on a level playing field. This is the theory.

In reality, standardized tests were used as a means to hold teachers and administrators accountable. Jobs in education depended on the test scores. If students at one school did not perform well, the entire school could be subject to changes in administration, transfer of teachers, or takeover by the state. If students in one class did not perform well, the teacher could be put on an action plan that could lead to termination. The stakes are set high, resulting in schools requiring teachers to teach to the test (although those specific words may not have been used). Teachers had no choice but to teach in this manner—their livelihoods depended upon it. As a result of the stress put on teachers, they in turn added stress to students by emphasizing the importance of students performing well. Unfortunately, many teachers would even threaten students with fear of failing a grade or going to summer school if they did not score well.

The sad, unspoken truth and overlooked reality is that not all children come to school prepared to learn. Poverty is a great problem in many societies, including ours. But perhaps the bigger problem is the number of students coming to school with more pressing problems. Homes of abusive parents, addicted parents, and ill-equipped grandparents, aunts, or uncles rearing children typically present problems that cannot be solved at school. In our efforts to climb to the top of the ladder, we have ignored the children living in homes that simply cannot help the students to further their education. Children are living in homes in fear of anger or an abusive outrage. Children are living in homes of single parents who may have health or addiction problems. And let us not forget the children who may be dealing with the death of a parent or sibling. These issues alone deter learning. With multiple stressors at hand, these children can easily fall behind.

In our efforts to report data and to brag about statistics, we have lost the human side of learning. Putting computer devices in front of children hardly compensates for the deep ache in their stomachs from the stress and dread of going home. Not scoring well on a test cannot compare with the knowledge that they are moving yet again because their parents cannot pay the bill. Our society has painted a great picture that all children come to school with the same home life and family values, but that is simply not true. We are made to believe all children appear at school with smiles on their faces, songs in their hearts, and a hardy appetite for learning. This is true for many children, but is false for even more.

Education is about more than teaching a test. It is about teaching character and showing children how to share and get along with one another. It is about allowing children to fail and encouraging them to try again. It is about teaching them to find a passion for learning and a passion for solving a problem. It is about instilling curiosity about the world in which we live and inspiring them to become valued assets to their community. Education is about the whole person, which cannot be measured by a simple test score.

Society (i.e., corporations and politicians) has told us it is imperative for our children to have the best education money can buy to compete in the workplace of the twenty-first century. We have been advised the path laid by these corporations and politicians is the best for the education of our children, although none of these people are educators or psychologists. The reality is they have their own greed and agendas driving them to influence society and parents, and these agendas are void of any real, reliable research to substantiate their claims.

START TAKING NOTES! PARENTS NEED TO KNOW THIS!

I was raised in a middle-class neighborhood, went to public school and community college, and then went to state-supported college. I later obtained a master's degree. All was completed without the aid of standardized tests or fancy computer programs and devices. The education system then was much simpler and, I dare say, more academic than we see today. Exams were not standardized. Instead, they were created by teachers or included with the textbooks. Every student did not have the same test, but all students were expected to learn the same information, which was delivered through a textbook. Accountability lay on the shoulders of the students. Retention was an actual possibility, which all students feared. It was unheard of for parents to complain to teachers and administrators for their own child's failures. Though not every teacher was an exceptional one (we had our share of disappointing teachers, just as every generation does), students were trusted to rely on their own resources to acquire the information they needed to obtain good grades. Students were more independent, more resourceful, and more confident in themselves and their abilities. Dependence on parents and blaming others for shortcomings was not an option. Now, students use Common Core Curriculum, which is the term used to name the new standards being implemented in most American schools.

I have briefly outlined how we have gotten from there to here.

- In the 1980s, education (specifically students, teachers, and schools) was blamed for the American decline in the world economy. (Baken, p.143)[1] This was a large burden to place on education.
- President Ronald Reagan released a report entitled *A Nation at Risk* in 1983. This report recommended changes in education to include more rigor, more homework, longer school days, longer school years, and standardized testing, which should be linked to teacher pay. (Baken, p.143)[2]
- President George H. W. Bush implemented No Child Left Behind (NCLB) in 2002, tying student performance in education to federal funds, requiring testing beginning in grade 3, and including higher standards. This has been attributed to the beginning of teachers teaching to the test. The pressure on student performance has grown exponentially in the following years.
- On February 17, 2009, President Barack Obama followed suit with his own plan, A Race to the Top, with the idea

schoolchildren should be preparing to work for corporations. (Baken, p.144)[3] This included even kindergarten students. The term "College- and Career-ready Standards" was soon heard in every classroom in America and discussed in parent conferences.

It is my personal belief that none of these moves were made with bad intentions. I believe each president had confidence in quick fixes and thought that the promoting companies could provide instant results. They had been elected to do a job and had an extremely limited time frame to accomplish results. I believe these were some of the most basic reasons presidents pushed this type of agenda. Unfortunately, once these were passed, our students were subjected to a new frontier and unchartered waters.

WHAT IS NOT PUBLIC KNOWLEDGE?

There is a monetary gold mine to be made by these testing corporations, which operate behind closed doors with little to no public accountability. "There's very little oversight of the testing industry," notes Walt Haney, an education professor at Boston College and a senior researcher at its National Board on Educational Testing and Public Policy (NBETPP). "In fact, there is more public oversight of the pet industry and the food we feed our dogs than there is for the quality of tests we make our kids take."[4]

"While the public knows little of the testing companies, lobbyists have ensured that legislators are well aware of those corporate interests. Following Bush's first election and his unveiling of NCLB, testing company representatives descended upon Congress, pushing for the type of standardized testing that Governor Bush had made so popular in Texas."[5]

"A January 2002 article in *The Nation* points out that the Bush administration has a particularly 'cozy relationship' with the testing company run by McGraw-Hill. The heart of this relationship, the article notes, 'lies the three-generation social mingling between the McGraw and Bush families. The McGraws are old Bush friends, dating back to the 1930s. In fact, on the first day he assumed his job at the White House, Bush invited Harold McGraw III into his office, according to *The Nation*.'"[6]

The major benefactors of these tests include McGraw-Hill, Pearson Educational Measurement, and Riverside Publishing. These popular testing companies may change slightly year to year or may be renamed over the years.

"The testing companies are driven by the need to make profits, not to improve education. They will do whatever the market requires them to do—nothing more, nothing less. 'These companies are really only interested in making money, and under NCLB they will make more money, while essentially remaining unaccountable,' notes Neil (Monty Neil, executive director of the Boston-based group FairTest). 'In other words, you keep the pain public, and you privatize the profits.'"[7]

Common Core testing has led to teachers being terminated and some principals and administrators being moved to other schools. Some schools have been closed or taken over by the state board of education. Education was no longer about the individual student; it was about test scores.

Video games have been found to be addictive, causing mental and physical harm to children. Reports from the Mayo Clinic and Frontiers in Psychology are just some of many stating these dangers. Yet this research is ignored, and video games are used and encouraged as a way to teach children. Many companies began developing educational video games to entice children to become consumers of their wares, and the younger, the better.

Research has found technology-based learning and interventions have produced lower improvement levels compared with more traditional methods.

Common Core focuses on reading informational books, resulting in children no longer reading simply for pleasure.

"No other nation in the world has inflicted so many changes or imposed so many mandates on its teachers and public schools as we have in the past dozen years. No other nation tests every student every year as we do. Our students are the most over-tested in the world. No other nation—at least no high-performing nation— judges the quality of teacher performance by the test scores of their students. Most researchers agree that this methodology is fundamentally flawed, that it is inaccurate, unreliable, and unstable. That the highest ratings will go to teachers with the most affluent students and the lowest ratings will go to teachers of English Language Learners, Exceptional Child teachers, and teachers in high poverty and low socio-economic areas."[8]

Due to complaints from many teachers about the unfairness of testing scores, many school systems altered the way scores were evaluated. Instead of defining progress based on the scores at the end of the year, many districts are now choosing to define progress based on the amount of growth a student has from one year to the next. Again, this is a flawed system for several reasons. The curriculum changes from grade to grade, and it is therefore unfair to judge based on new content. One student may understand decimals and fractions well but may have difficulty understanding algebraic concepts of solving for an unknown variable. This fundamentally goes against student learning levels, which develop at varying rates. Another problem with this evaluation method is once students reach a level of 90–95 percent efficiency, it is hard for them to grow. In fact, this group of students tends to reach a plateau, level off, and decline slightly before rising to a new height. This is comparable to a teacher telling students they will have to consistently make 96 or above on every test to show growth.

And then there is the common problem of middle school students when they reach puberty. Their focus turns to their peers and relationships and away from academics, before often returning their attention to academics in high school. As you see, there is not one easy system to use standardized test scores as a means to evaluate all students for growth or proficiency.

"The Common Core standards were written in 2009 under the aegis of several Washington, D.C.–based organizations: The National Governors Association, The Council of Chief State School Officers, and Achieve. The development process was left behind closed doors and led by a small organization called Student Achievement Partners, headed by David Coleman. The writing group of 27 contained few educators, but a significant number of representatives of the testing industry. From the onset, the Common Core standards were marked by the absence of public participation, transparency, or educator participation. In a democracy, transparency is crucial because transparency and openness build trust. Those crucial ingredients were lacking."[9]

HOW EDUCATION MONEY IS SPENT

Common Core has been a money-making method for testing companies, computers, and technology device makers, including the high-tech smartboard industry and companies providing the bandwidth needed for children to access online learning and testing. All these companies are profiting from the constant use of technology in the schools.

"Standardized testing is a profitable and growing industry. No Child Left Behind created a demand for 45 million tests to be produced and graded each year and accounted for a full third of the $3 billion revenue generated by the testing industry in 2008." (Bakan, p.158)[10]

> Dear Jesus,
> You who promise to be with me always, I pray that You will be with my children today as they go to school. Bless their going and their coming. Bless their learning and their playing. Please protect their hearts from fear. Please keep them safe. Please give them good friends. Give them joy this day. Thank You for loving them from head to toe. In Your name, amen.

Sylvia McCrory

THE LOS ANGELES FIASCO

"Los Angeles alone committed to spend $1 billion on iPads for student testing, the money is being taken from a bond issue approved by voters for construction and repair of school facilities. Meanwhile, the district has cut teachers of the arts, class size has increased, and necessary repairs are deferred because the money will be spent on iPads. The iPads will be obsolete in a year or two, and the Pearson content loaded onto the iPads has only a three-year license. The cost of implementing the Common Core and the new tests is likely to run into the billions at a time of deep budget cuts."[11] But this is not the end of the story.

The superintendent of Los Angeles Unified School District, John Deasy, wanted all 650,000 students in his district to have "an iPad loaded with educational software goodies from Pearson" at a cost of $1.3 billion. With much hype, propaganda, and faith in the testing process being touted, the iPads were approved by the school board and were purchased. The outcome has led to an FBI investigation.

> The Pearson platform had an incomplete curriculum that was essentially worthless, and the tablets themselves were easily hacked within weeks by students who bypassed the feeble security restrictions and were able to freely surf the Internet—video games and porn for everyone! The whole deal was killed in December 2014—the day after the FBI seized twenty boxes of documents from the district's business office as part of its investigation into the contract with Apple. Under scrutiny were the bidding process and the relationship between Superintendent John Deasy—who resigned abruptly under pressure in October 2014—and his close relationship with Apple and Pearson executives, the beneficiaries of the mammoth contract. (Kardaras, pp.209-10)[12]

NEW YORK CITY SCHOOLS: JOEL KLEIN AND RUPERT MURDOCH

One of many stories revealing that greed is the driving factor of many decisions being made in education is the story of New York City School and Joel Klein. Much like the private industry, the decision-makers, executives, and leaders are turning a profit at the expense of the workers (teachers and staff) and the students.

In 2002, Mayor Michael Bloomberg appointed Joel Klein as chancellor of New York City Schools, overseeing the education of 1.1 million students. Klein went to Harvard, was an attorney, had served as assistant attorney general in charge of the Anti-Trust Division under Bill Clinton, and was later appointed as a US assistant attorney general in the Department of Justice. He had no background in education, had never taught school, had no experience working in education. But he was appointed to manage the learning of a million students.

In 2007, Klein spent $95 million taxpayer dollars on "the implementation of ARIS (Achievement Reporting and Innovation System), a data collection and student tracking computer system. ARIS immediately got blasted by critics, teachers, and parents as being slow, clunky, and largely unutilized. Klein then awarded the internet start-up company, Wireless Generation, a $12 million annual contract to fix and maintain his broken and expensive clunker." (Kardaras, p.198)[13]

Klein had an annual salary of $225,000 with the school system. He resigned from that position to take a $2 million per year salary with Amplify (formerly called Wireless Generation), owned by Rupert Murdoch, which included a $1 million signing bonus. To recap: Klein created a problem, was paid to fix the problem, and then was hired to run the company fixing the problem he had created.

"Murdoch had invested almost a billion dollars in Amplify in pursuit of the educational holy grail—an Amplify tablet (for only $199!) in the hands of every student in America" (Kardaras, p.198)[14] Are you seeing, as I am, that there is no interest in the education or welfare of children in any of this?

What Murdoch saw was "a company that could create a tablet that could be programmed with all this new Common Core goodness which would make textbooks obsolete—and all with an annual licensing fee. Ka-ching!" Eventually, New York City Schools abandoned the ARIS program. Amplify was bleeding money. Murdoch sold it to Klein, and Klein is trying to turn it around. (Kardaras p.200)[15] And what about the students? Reports indicated the students using the technology scored lower than their peers not using technology. (Kardaras, p.202)[16] I have lost count. Have you been keeping a tally of the money wasted and given to high-paid executives? How have we become so blind and trusting of these individuals and their rhetoric, and yet we have little faith in the people and teachers we know and see?

"The sad reality is that companies like Apple and Pearson are profit-driven entities whose mission statement is to increase the bottom line. I think we all understand that this is America and that companies should be allowed to make profits, but they should not do so at the expense of children's well-being. There should be extra scrutiny and vetting before schools get in bed with for-profit companies, because, unfortunately, those companies don't always have the best interests of the kids in mind." Two executives from Houghton Mifflin Harcourt were recorded by "James O'Keefe of Project Veritas, a nonprofit that investigates public- and private-sector misconduct and fraud. In the hidden-cam videos, the cynical executives are caught discussing the Common Core and their concern---or lack thereof---for what's best for kids. You don't think that the educational publishing companies are in it for education, do you? No. They're in it for the money," Dianne Barrow, the West Coast accounts manager for Houghton Mifflin Harcourt, was caught on camera saying. After explaining that Common Core is overwhelmingly profit-driven, Barrow went on to say, "I hate kids. I'm in it to sell books. Don't even kid yourself for a heartbeat,' she says as she starts to laugh hysterically."

Another Houghton Mifflin executive, strategic account manager Amelia Petties, had this to say in a conversation about the Common Core that was captured by a hidden camera: "'Common Core is not new. We are calling it Common Core, woohoo! Call it Common Core … there's always money in it because kids are great but it's not always about the kids.' She pauses, then says, 'It's never about the kids,' as she breaks out into loud cackling laughter." (Kardaras, p.213)[17]

Some will not be shocked or offended by these comments, possibly considering them simply part of business. But would you want your children's education determined and manipulated by private, profit-driven companies that display contempt for kids and their education?

COMMON CORE AND TEACHER EVALUATIONS

Unlike previous generations, teachers in America do not have the freedom or flexibility to teach in the way they find is best for their students. Teachers in schools where Common Core is used are evaluated according to a rubric. These evaluations are conducted through observations by administrators and may be unannounced. With that in mind, teachers must be always on their guard, implementing all the standards every minute of every day. These evaluations can push the teachers to perform in a manner that may not be in the best interests of the students or reflect how they would teach without this constant pressure. Teachers not performing well on evaluations could be placed on an action plan or lose their jobs.

With many textbooks outdated and no longer available, teachers must look to online resources to find curriculum-related materials. This was originally a good idea, but it has become a waste of valuable time for many. Teachers can certainly find good ideas online; there is no question there. The problem arises when teachers of different grade levels are pulling from the same resource. For example, a third-grade teacher may find material she feels is appropriate for her third graders, and a fourth-grade teacher may prepare lessons based on the same materials only to find the students have already used this resource the previous year. Instead of teachers working together to help each other, the high-stakes testing has resulted in some teachers working independently and against each other. Everyone wants to have the highest test scores, making some teachers secretive about good ideas and strategies. This is an unfortunate reality.

Legislators, government leaders, and business executives have decided to view education as a business enterprise. Evaluations of teachers and students determine whether teachers continue to work, whether schools stay open, and whether students are promoted or are required to attend summer school. For years, the blame for the decline in American education has fallen in the wrong place. All the ills of education have been placed at the doors of the teachers, the individuals who can really impact the lives of students and therefore the future of our society. No longer are teachers afforded the freedom to teach to their students based on the abilities, inabilities, and needs of children as broad as the spectrum of diversity in society. Teachers are expected to mold every student in the classroom into the same mold by the end of the year. No longer are teachers treated as professionals with experience, knowledge, and understanding of the challenges students face in today's world. Instead, teachers are considered merely bodies in a classroom, and they are expected to prepare students for the workforce of the future even though no one knows what advances that future will hold.

> Research shows that you begin learning in the womb and go right on learning until the moment you pass on. Your brain has a capacity for learning that is virtually limitless, which makes every human a potential genius.
> —Michael J. Gelb

STANDARDIZED TESTING IS THE ANSWER FOR PUBLIC SCHOOL STUDENTS BUT IS NOT GOOD ENOUGH FOR THEIR CHILDREN

Wait! In American schools, students are expected to take standardized tests, which often include progress testing throughout the year. But the very people touting the benefits of standardized testing will not allow their children to be subject to the same stress and scrutiny. Wow!

Former President Barack Obama and his wife, Michelle Obama, sent their daughters to Sidwell Friends School in Washington, DC, a private Quaker school. The philosophy of the school is "progressive and child-centered: 'We are committed to the joys of exploration and discovery.' Students neither sit for any standardized tests nor are teachers' evaluations tied to test scores. 'The curriculum provides a broad foundation in the humanities and sciences, develops critical and creative thinking, stresses competence in oral and written communication and quantitative operations, and stimulates intellectual curiosity.'"[18] President Joe Biden's grandchildren also attended Sidwell Friends School. The class size is much smaller than public schools, with a ratio of ten to twelve students for each teacher.[19]

The list of parents sending their children to private, elite schools where standardized testing does not exist includes many politicians, the wealthy, celebrities, and supporters of standardized testing. So why are we so quick to be sold on these tests and standards if they are not acceptable to the very people creating and mandating them?

The intention to find a fast, easy way to use testing scores to find the best teachers was not meant to be detrimental, but technology and a test cannot measure the heart of a teacher. The security a child feels with a teacher or the bond between the teacher and student is treasured in this profession. Ironically, many of the Silicon Valley tech executives do not use the same standards to judge their children's teachers. In fact, they send their children to the Waldorf School.

WHAT IS THE WALDORF SCHOOL?

According to their website:

> Waldorf teachers appreciate that technology must assume a role in education, but at the appropriate developmental stage, when a young person has reached the intellectual maturity to reason abstractly and process concretely on his or her own, which is at around the age of 14. Society might challenge this principle, as many young children are well able to complete sophisticated tasks on

a computer; the Waldorf perspective is that computer exposure should not be based on capability but on developmental appropriateness. While many applaud adult-like thinking in young children, we observe that a child's natural, instinctive, creative, and curious way of relating to the world may be repressed when technology is introduced into the learning environment at an early age.[20]

PERSONAL REFLECTION

The private schools chosen by the very people promoting and mandating Common Core and standardized testing do not implement them. Their schools encourage children to think abstractly and encourage higher-level thinking. They discourage the use of computers for education until the age of fourteen. They treat children like children, not mini adults, and they do not push children to prepare for the adult world. They are allowing children to grow and develop the way God intended. They encourage time for natural curiosity and creativity. They are not worried about comparing children with test scores. But we are. Why?

THE PHILOSOPHY ABOUT GRADING
AND STANDARDIZED TESTING

Assessment may vary slightly from school to school, but in most cases, a full assessment of each student's progress is provided in the form of a year-end narrative assessment in all subject areas. These assessments are supported by teacher conferences and class meetings throughout the year. In high school, GPAs are included in unofficial transcripts to indicate a student's academic standing to colleges and universities. We believe that standardized testing is not an accurate or complete reflection of a student's knowledge, intellectual capacities, or ability to learn. Thus, our curriculum does not put the focus on standardized test-taking preparation, particularly in the lower and middle grades. In high school, SAT and ACT preparation courses may be offered.[21]

Here is the big question: If standardized testing is not good enough for politicians' children and the children of its advocates, why should it be good enough for our children?

The American education system has only gotten worse since the implementation of Common Core and standardized testing. It is linked to teacher evaluations in every grade level from kindergarten to twelfth grade. Our politicians continue to support it and pour more taxpayer money into it, but they do not support this system enough to subject their own children to it. Yet we are to use it as our guide for our children and their successes and failures. This looks like a red flag to me.

Why not invest in research and pilot programs to simulate the same philosophy that is used with the schools of the Silicon Valley children? If the Obamas felt a school without standardized testing is best for their girls, why not push for the implementation of similar teaching and evaluation of all American students? The same question applies to all politicians and powers that be who determine the education of public school students. If the system they are touting is so great, why is it not appropriate for their children?

THE UNSPOKEN PROBLEM

The legislators, government, and businesses refuse to recognize children cannot be treated as inanimate objects. Children are living, breathing human beings created by God and designed to be individuals with unique God-given gifts. Children are curious and want to please from the time they are toddlers into elementary school. But not all children are born into the same environment. Some do not have kind, loving parents or the attention they need to thrive. Many live with socioeconomic challenges within areas where they are required to attend low-performing schools. Many live with addiction and abuse within their family.

During my teaching career, I encountered many families with happy homes, but also many unhealthy home environments. In most of these situations, the children and parents keep the home environment hidden. Children who grow up in abusive situations do not know any other way of life. For many children, the abuse is not physical but psychological. Homes with addicted parents, poverty, or illegal immigrants are often filled with stress, anger, and worry. Children are easy targets for adults' unhappiness, fears, and frustrations.

As a teacher, I have taught children living with older siblings, grandparents, or great-grandparents; children living in foster homes; and children who spent their weekends visiting one of their parents in prison. As much as we would like to believe all children live in happy, supportive homes, that is just not the truth.

My fear is for all children, but those with unstable home lives are more likely to imitate the behaviors they have observed at home. There are no healthy role models for these children. Education is not important; survival is urgent and requires their attention.

This was a few decades ago, before the Internet, cell phones, tablets, and laptop computers were so commonplace. Imagine what the home lives of students like these are today, especially with the rise of heroin, fentanyl, and opioids in our country. I question the logic of those who think these children and children like them are concerned about grades, their future, or eventual careers. They must first feel safe and secure in their homes, realize their worth, and above all learn to love themselves. Students like this may not have been shown many expressions of love and concern from those who are supposed to love and care for them. Unfortunately, I could go on with more stories about students like these. No one likes to think about this side of education or the children who need more attention than learning basic skills.

There are children born with learning and emotional problems due to the addiction of mothers when pregnant. There are children in schools who are addicted to drugs, on probation, and abused both physically and sexually. Some children have become gang members with aspirations of violence and illegal activity, seeing this as the only way to earn money and survive.

One segment of the student demographic is "revolving door students." They live with family members for a few months and then are sent to live in another city, often another state with other family members, only to return later where the cycle continues. Not only do these students have a hard time adjusting to changing schools, friends, and keeping up with missed assignments, but they do not feel like they belong anywhere.

> Good works do not make a good man, but a good man
> does good works.
> —Martin Luther

WHAT ABOUT THE FAMILY'S ROLE IN EDUCATION?

Families are failing their own children with the expectation that schools will raise their children and correct any problems their children display. The public would not believe how many times teachers are told by parents in conferences that they are responsible for this, because taxes are paid for teachers to teach. For many of these students, the problems they have are too painful, and the hurt is too deep for the teachers to be allowed to break through the wall the students have created in order to protect themselves. There are counselors at the schools who make numerous attempts to reach these students. However, students understand teachers and counselors are not family and will not be part of their lives forever. Therein lies the appeal of gangs, sex, and drugs.

Do not make assumptions these are only the children from the lower socioeconomic groups. It occurs in all groups and in every level of society, from the poorest to the richest and from the least educated to the highly educated. A sense of being safe and loved and of belonging is vital for all of us, especially children.

Sylvia McCrory

THE BIG IGNORED PROBLEM

People who are not involved in public education or who do not work with schoolchildren have the misconception that all children arrive at school wanting to learn, are eager to be there, do their assignments on time, and study for tests. This is often the exception, as few children are self-motivated today. Children view education as a by-product of school. Many children of all ages enjoy the social aspect of the school. Some children are pleasing parents and teachers, whereas others are there because state laws require them to be. Then there are the students there because parents need childcare and view school as the babysitter.

This is probably the single most important reason American children are falling behind other countries. Neither parents nor children view education as an opportunity or value the ability to attend school for the purpose of learning.

Many of the children's homes are more than unstable. Socioeconomic disparities have been blamed for many educational problems. I am not disagreeing or questioning this conclusion, but the lack of parental respect for the teaching profession and the failure to recognize and instill a work ethic in children is more damaging to education than any other factor.

Brian was a student from a low-economic area, but his mother was a strong, determined lady. She had respect for the education system and understood this was the way for Brian to become a better person. She did not allow her son to veer too far from the path of education. He was my student in eighth grade. By junior year in high school, he worked part-time in a supermarket, played on the football team, and was taking honors classes while working on an academic scholarship. He told me all about this when I went to the supermarket and discovered him at work one evening.

It has been my experience in teaching many children from mostly higher socioeconomic backgrounds with professional parents that they are given every advantage possible. Some of these students have performed well, but there are many who have lacked motivation or discipline to excel. Instead, they act out at school, seeking the attention they do not get at home. Some of these parents have become unavailable due to career obligations, creating a void in the family.

Contrary to popular belief, many American children are pampered and spoiled. They make many family decisions, such as what they will eat for dinner, where the family will go on vacation, and even which rewards and privileges they are entitled. Instead of these instances making children happier and more secure, it has created children who are insecure, unhealthy, and without direction or motivation. When parents give children everything they want, they have no goals for which to work. Without realizing it, some parents have robbed their children of one of the most vital needs for happiness. These parents are no longer giving their children a purpose. Our purpose is the reason we get up in the mornings and do our jobs. It is what drives us each day. Children who are given everything have nothing to drive them and no reason to excel. When children are young, they are driven by wanting to please their parents. By middle school, children begin to pull away from their parents and cling to their peers. It is during these years that children need to be self-motivated. They need a purpose that is completely their own. For children without a purpose, they are lost and seek short-term, worthless goals such as getting to the next level of a video game or seeing how far they can push the limits at home or school. I encourage parents to avoid showing love to their children through material gifts. Teach children early on how to set goals, develop a plan, and reap the rewards of their accomplishment.

Unlike previous generations, where children were expected to take on chores and responsibilities without pay (and were expected to eat the food set before them), parents today have given children the role of adults. In reality, Christian parenthood requires that parents guide, lead, and become models for what adulthood should be.

Parents, family, and home life play a large part in student learning. Too many times, the whole child—mental health, values, personality— is ignored when it is perhaps the single most important reason children may succeed in school. More than the socioeconomic factor, it is the attitude of parents toward education, their confidence to parent as an adult, their value of learning, and their support of the teacher that impacts the success or failure of children.

> Let no Christian parents fall into the delusion that Sunday School is intended to ease them of their personal duties. The first and most natural condition of things is for Christian parents to train up their own children in the nurture and admonition of the Lord.
> —Charles Haddon Spurgeon

TAKEAWAYS

- America as well as many other countries have become obsessed with greed and instant gratification.
- We have become a data-driven culture. We have a need for concrete numbers to prove "I am better than you."
- Standardized testing provides a means for students and teachers to be evaluated.
- Common Core strives to tie every student to the Internet and digital world in preparation for the adult world.
- The mandating of Common Core and standardized testing has generated billions of dollars for technology and software companies. These tax dollars also help drive the economy.
- Theory is not the same as reality, especially when dealing with children.
- Many of those mandating and creating standardized testing do not advocate it enough to send their own children to schools where it is implemented.
- American children are the most tested in the world, yet it has not improved their education.
- Standardized testing and Common Core have removed the time necessary for children to be children from classroom schedules.

- The private schools attended by the biggest proponents of standardized testing and Common Core do not advocate the use of computers for students until the age of fourteen. The philosophy is children are born with "natural, instinctive, creative and curious ways of relating to the world" that "may be repressed when technology is introduced into the learning environment at an early age."

REFERENCES FOR CHAPTER 1

1   J. Bakan, *Childhood under Siege: How Big Business Ruthlessly Targets Children* (New York: Free, 2011).
2   Ibid.
3   Ibid.
4   Barbara Miner, "Testing Companies Mine for Gold," October 22, 2020, accessed November 05, 2020, https://rethinkingschools.org/articles/keeping-public-schools-public-testing-companies-mine-for-gold/. Barbara Miner (barbaraminer@ameritech.net) is a freelance writer and former managing editor of *Rethinking Schools*.
5   Ibid.
6   Ibid.
7   Ibid.,
8   V. Strauss, "Everything You Need to Know about Common Core—Ravitch," April 24, 2019, accessed November 06, 2020, https://www.washingtonpost.com/news/answer-sheet/wp/2014/01/18/everything-you-need-to-know-about-common-core-ravitch/.
9   Ibid.
10 J. Bakan, *Childhood under Siege*.
11 V. Strauss, "Everything You Need to Know about Common Core."
12 N. Kardaras, *Glow Kids* (New York: St. Martin's, 2016).
13 Ibid.
14 Ibid.
15 Ibid.
16 Ibid.
17 Ibid.
18 N. Goyal, "These Politicians Think Your Kids Need High-Stakes Testing—but Not Theirs," April 6, 2016, accessed November 18, 2020, https://www.thenation.com/article/archive/these-politicians-think-your-kids-need-high-stakes-testing-but-not-theirs/.

19 Ibid.

20 "FAQs about Waldorf," accessed November 19, 2020, https://www.waldorfeducation.org/waldorf-education/faqs-about-waldorf.

21 Ibid.

CHAPTER 2

The Internet and Our Brains

> Those who live according to the sinful nature have their minds set on what that nature desires, but those who live in accordance with the Spirit have their minds set on what the Spirit desires. The mind of sinful man is death, but the mind controlled by the Spirit is life and peace; the sinful mind is hostile to God. It does not submit to God's law, nor can it do so. Those controlled by sinful nature cannot please God. (Romans 8:5–8 NIV)

Let's take a look at the workings of our brains. As we explore this subject, I encourage you to focus on the ways our brains are becoming altered.

The brain "controls our ability to think, talk, feel, see, hear, remember things, walk, and much more. It even controls our breathing".[22] The brain has three main parts: the cerebrum, the cerebellum, and the brain stem. Within the cerebrum are two hemispheres. "Each hemisphere has four sections, called lobes: frontal, parietal, temporal, and occipital. Each lobe controls specific functions. For example, the frontal lobe controls personality, decision-making, and reasoning, while the temporal lobe controls, memory speech, and sense of smell."[23]

I start with this brief explanation of the brain to point out just a few of the functions of the frontal lobe of the brain. It controls our decision-making, reasoning, and personality. I would like each of you reading this to keep this in mind and refer back to it as we study our current education system.

Parents today consider themselves an involved and educated civilization. Young parents should be applauded because they are concerned about the well-being of future generations. People no longer want chemicals in their bodies unless absolutely necessary. Taking unnecessary medicine is frowned upon. Parents today do not give children medicine or food without knowing whether it is safe, has been tested, and is the right amount to give. Children are not allowed to play on unsafe playgrounds; the equipment must be proven safe, anchored well, and free of any dangers. We now live in a society that seeks healthy living, getting lots of exercise, and watching our diet. We want only the safest products for our families.

Therefore, I am saddened that these same people allow and encourage children to stay constantly connected to the Internet without researching the effects. A company inserting the word *educational* on a computer game puts that game in the must-have category for many families. Parents are constantly being fed false information. They are being told their children will be "behind" if they do not stay updated with the most advanced technological devices and programs. Yet the research is still out. Children are being subjected to the biggest experiment of all time.

Here is where I want parents to be cautious. The whole world is practically throwing technology in our faces. We are seeing wonderful, amazing things technology can do, but we tend to believe the bad things about technology happen only to others. Are we deceiving ourselves?

Naomi Schaefer Riley, in *Be the Parent, Please*, writes,

> Lowell Monke, a professor of education at Wittenberg University, has written extensively on the relationship between technology and learning. Parents, he tells me, "are so proud of how their kids can handle this incredibly complicated stuff and so worried their kids will fall behind because that's what the future is all about." Even if parents worry about screen time, he says, they have a

"religious reverence for technology. We fear it, but in the long run, we believe in it." (Riley, pp.53-4)[24]

Riley explains the attraction children have with the bright, shiny buttons. Even infants are handed iPads, iPhones, or other devices to entertain them and occupy their time. Parents are bragging about how much their children are learning, but children are not interested in correct answers; they simply enjoy pressing the shiny objects on the screen. (Riley, p.58)[25]

This is where I would like to add some food for thought. Before I do, please understand I most likely would have been taken in by these devices if my children had been young when they became available. Think of it this way: children, and even infants, love the distractions of the shiny screens because it amuses them. Parents now are free to get some necessary housework completed or devote time to another child. But if this distraction had been something else, like an abundance of candy or ice cream, would we have allowed our children to have them continually, or even every day? Now, what if these devices are determined to be more dangerous to children than obesity or diabetes?

Comparisons with addiction to devices and gambling addiction are currently being studied. The findings are not encouraging for technology-minded parents. Gamblers playing slot machines have been studied for many years, and research has discovered that after a while, gamblers are no longer interested in winning or losing. They are connected to the machine and the addiction to the roll of the fruit. This is much the same way people playing *Candy Crush*, or another game, are so focused on continuing: they are unaware of their surroundings. No one is learning anything. There are no skills. The game has trapped the player. (Riley, p.59)[26]

Most parents understand this concept. As long as children are allowed to stay connected to their devices, there is usually peace. However, the moment the device is removed, the child is not happy to be disconnected. Then what? Does the child become like a gambler or addict, having withdrawal from technology? This is a real thing. It is happening in more and more families every day.

According to Riley,

> Educational technology may seem to be a vehicle for giving young children a leg up on their peers, but it may put them at a disadvantage developmentally. They are losing out on an important way to learn, to give their minds appropriate rest, and to give their bodies an appropriate outlet.

> And while it may seem as though our children can gain more academic skills through educational software; it is also possible that these touchscreen and button-pushing activities are inhibiting them socially and intellectually. We are habituating them toward activities with predictable outcomes. Over time, they may become more drawn to these activities because they are easier than the alternative—trying to navigate new social situations or exploring new physical environments. (Riley, pp.168-9)[27]

What about human interactions? We need to assess ourselves and our children to be sure we are making time for each other. Are we becoming so comfortable on the web that we are avoiding human contact? Even during COVID-19, a phone call is better with actual voices than texting. Have our children begun to talk to strangers online? Is it easier to play a game online than in person with friends? How much time are we spending online? These are all warning signs of bigger dangers ahead.

The fast-paced explosion of the Internet into our lives has created a world with little time to gather information about its effects on our brains. After all, when the family home desktop computer was first introduced to most Americans in the early 1980s, the Internet was foreign and still unavailable to most. There were many who wondered how we would use these computers and whether it was only an expensive device to perform a limited number of tasks. Then as the Internet was developed and Google created a platform for us to find information quickly, we all fell in love with the Internet and our computer systems. No one suspected any problems or any downsides to this wonderful world of information.

As the devices became smaller and cheaper, more and more people bought them and used them consistently. We were swept into a new world of constant information at our fingertips. Before long, a new system of communication was developed, something originally created to stay in touch with friends. It quickly evolved into a way to communicate with the world: social media. Suddenly everyone, including infants and toddlers, were tuned in to their computers and devices.

Now, here we are in 2021 with more research and more information about this fairly new phenomenon. All along the way, we have discovered some alarming facts about our brains and the Internet. The research has been reported here and there, but not enough for us to really take notice—until now. The question is whether we are so consumed by this wonderful world that we ignore the warnings. Our brains are the control center of our bodies, relaying messages to other parts of our bodies that range from physical pain to emotional happiness.

Perhaps more alarming is the addiction parents have to the Internet and their unwillingness to disconnect themselves. I think most of us have observed parents on their phones or devices, ignoring a child trying to get their attention. Has this become who we are? Are we telling our children this device is more important than they are?

We all need human contact, especially children. Learning from a machine is limiting at best. Children do not learn how to negotiate, how to compromise, or how to fit into the real world through a device. A machine does not teach children how to love others or how to care for someone. It does not have hurt feelings, so it cannot teach children how to repair a wrong they may have done to someone. A machine cannot teach children they will not always be first, they will not always be winners, they will not always be tested by knowledge, but sometimes they will be tested for kindness and compassion to others.

Although our focus of this book is on children and youth, please recognize and understand the dangers to adults. My point is to highlight how easily we take for granted the health of our brains. If we can avoid harming our brains, it is to our advantage to do everything possible to keep them healthy. Remember, the frontal lobe of the brain controls our decision-making, reasoning, and personality. We must be careful to protect this area of our brains and of our children's brains. It is vital that we spend more time working with our children to develop healthy brains. This will often involve more work from parents and more personal interaction. The most difficult job for parents will be to disconnect from the Internet frequently, allowing it to be used only at specific times and only for specific activities. Our children learn more from what we do than what we say.

> O Lord our God, we gather together today to give You thanks and praise Your greatness. We praise Your mighty works to the whole world. We praise You for Your wonderful deeds. Your power is limitless, Your wisdom is unparalleled, Your grace is overwhelming, and Your love is never failing. You promised that You will never leave or forsake us. Let us worship You in spirit and truth. Through Jesus Christ, our Lord, amen.

MORE INFORMATION ON THE BRAIN

It has long been believed that the brain develops gradually from the time a person is born until they reach adulthood. The belief has been that once we reach adulthood, our brains become hardwired. We have the capability of having new memories or storing new information. It was once thought that after maturity, the brain slowly deteriorates.

Researchers are now finding that to be false. I am not a scientist, so it is best to describe this in the words of others.

> Inside our skulls, they discovered, are some 100 billion neurons which take many different shapes and range in length from a few tenths of a millimeter to a few feet. A

single neuron typically has many dendrites (though only one axon), and dendrites and axons can have a multitude of branches and synaptic terminals. The average neuron makes about a thousand synaptic connections and some neurons can make a hundred times that number. The thousands of billions of synapses inside our skulls tie our neurons together into a dense mesh of circuits that, in ways that are still far from understood, give rise to what we think, how we feel, and who we are. (Carr, p.20)[28]

In his book *The Shallows: What the Internet Is Doing to Our Brains*, Nicholas Carr further explains the progression of research by biologists, psychologists, and neuroscientists, relating this to current research and findings. What has been discovered is unlike previous beliefs, according to Carr. The brain is not hardwired but has plasticity.

The adult brain, it turns out, is not just plastic but, as James Olds, a professor of neuroscience who directs the Krasnow Institute for Advanced Study at George Mason University, puts it, "very plastic." Our neurons are always breaking old connections and forming new ones, and brand-new nerve cells are always being created. "The brain," observes Olds, "has the ability to reprogram itself on the fly, altering the way it functions."(Carr, pp.26-7)[29]

Put in layman's terms, our brains have plasticity that allows constant change throughout our lifetimes. We are affected by external experiences in our brains. Some of these experiences will reward our brains, whereas others will signal depression and a change in our responses and behaviors. For example, if our brain is receiving a feeling of pleasure or reward, the behavior responsible for that will likely trigger our brain to seek it out. This is another warning of how the brain has the ability to change.

We are careful what we put into our bodies because we are aware of the long-term effects of overeating or eating the wrong foods. Do we take the time to think about the long-term effects of what is going into the brains of children? If a big chocolate cake was labeled healthy, would we allow our children to eat it all? What about if the cake company had a report certifying it to be healthy? Would we believe it? Or would we question it?

THE IMPORTANCE OF CONCENTRATION

Reading a book on paper requires concentration. It requires training our brains to ignore all distractions and focus on the written word. "In the quiet spaces opened up by the prolonged, undistracted reading of a book, people made their own associations, drew their own inferences and analogies, fostered their own ideas. They thought deeply as they read deeply."(Carr,p.65)[30]

Reading a book is a process requiring deep thought. It requires the reader to focus fully on the material and to become engaged with the words, characters, facts, and emotions poured out before them. It requires concentration on the pages in front of them as their mind is being filled. Reading a book removes distractions, replacing them with deep thought and focus. It equips us with margins for writing reflections, thoughts, ideas, and drawing diagrams, and sketches. "By allowing us to filter out distractions, to quiet the problem-solving functions of the frontal lobes, deep reading becomes a form of deep thinking. The mind of the experienced book reader is a calm mind, not a buzzing one. When it comes to the firing of our neurons, it's a mistake to assume that more is better."(Carr, pp.128-9)[31] In other words, it is possible to overstimulate our brains.

A book provides a sense of permanence. The words and thoughts recorded will always be in the same location. Returning to the book can be like returning to an old friend, where the characters come alive and bring memories or connections with it. A book can provide us with security, knowing it will always be there, along with the feelings and emotions associated with it.

So if the concentration is the act of mentally removing distractions to focus on a subject, isn't that what we want to do and teach our children to do when they read a text? Isn't our goal for our children to be able to retain information and apply it when necessary? Keep these thoughts in mind as we delve deeper into this information.

WHY THE EMPHASIS ON READING?

With the world becoming more digital, with more podcasts and more audiobooks, exactly what is all the fuss about concentration and reading? Although these are popular forms of communication and used frequently in today's culture, they have been found to have the ability to supply us only with short-term memory information. In other words, the most used forms of obtaining information today are presented in ways our brains can put only into our short-term memory. For entertainment or information, we may only want to distract or amuse ourselves. These are excellent modes of communication, but they lack the basics our brains depend on for developing long-term memory.

A word of caution for all reading: If your child is very young and reading on an advanced reading level, please screen their reading. Much of the content for advanced levels is for fifth grade and older and not meant for younger eyes. There are many valuable tools for you to use. A great place to start is commonsensemedia.org, with book reviews evaluating for appropriateness by age level. Evaluators even mention whether the book contains language or subject concerns. Also, consider supporting publishers who work to assist children and parents in locating appropriate reading based on a Christian lifestyle. One such new company for young adult novels is Clean Teen Publishing, with disclosures about the contents of their books. If parents research, lots of appropriate material is available. Be sure to share these resources with other parents, too.

THE HUGE PROBLEM

Children, especially in America, are expected to acquire their information through digital or computer-generated texts. Most textbooks and assignments are now only available digitally, especially during the COVID-19 pandemic. I understand all of the conveniences and the cost savings of digital information. I also understand the ease of laptops and tablets being so much more compact and lightweight than textbooks. There is no disputing that digital information and learning has its advantages. However, parents and teachers should know there are times when it is not the best choice. Going against the current trend may be difficult, but we need to weigh the options and decide how willing we are to carve the best route for our children, even if it is an old path that has been forgotten and worn over.

A digital book is not a physical book, and the choice for one over the other is deeply personal. In order to read it, one must scroll through it bit by bit. There are no pages to turn. The brain does not have any sense of the location of the information. For example, if the important information I need is in the last third of the book and in the middle of the page, my brain has no reference to imprint the important information any differently from the insignificant information. Our brain struggles to remember how to locate and retain vital information. The missing visual cues are draining our brains.

Researchers have found students reading from a computer or other digital device compared with students reading from books perform the same on short-term memory tests. However, when a test is given at a later date that relies on the development of long-term memories, the students reading from books performed much better.[32]

A study was done at West Point in 2016 by Susan Payne Carter, Kyle Greenberg, and Michael Walker. They found "the use of technology hurt academic performance. On the final exam, students in the sections that allowed some form of device use, scored 18 percent of a standard deviation lower than students in the section where devices were banned. Given that the exam counted for a quarter of the course grade, these differences could certainly mean the difference between passing and failing, the professors noted." (Riley,p.123-4)[33]

An article in the journal *Psychological Science* reports that even when students use laptops exclusively for the purpose of taking notes in class, they still performed worse than the students using the old-fashioned way of writing notes by hand. It was found that when students use laptops, they tend to take notes verbatim without regard to the words they are using and are not giving much thought to the content. Whereas students handwriting notes without the capacity to write as rapidly "listen, digest, and summarize so that they can succinctly capture the essence of the information. Thus, taking notes by hand forces the brain to engage in some heavy 'mental lifting,' and these efforts foster comprehension and retention." (Riley, p.125)[34]

In addition, we should not disregard the number of distractions students encounter when using the internet. Whether students are using textbooks or doing research online, there are, embedded within the text, links to other sites for additional information. Students following these links or glancing at the advertisements will no doubt lose their train of thought as they stray from their text. If this link is online, there will almost certainly be links, videos, or advertisements in the margins that are even more distracting for students. These distractions are there to remind students they must buy a new product or learn something new. But they must stay connected at all costs.

But there is more. Constantly popping up on the screen are Facebook notifications, emails, or Twitter alerts notifying students of incoming messages. As Carr points out, "We don't see the forest when we search the Web. We do not even see the trees. We see twigs and leaves. As companies like Google and Microsoft perfect search engines for video and audio content, more products are undergoing the fragmentation that already characterizes written works." (Carr p.91)[35]

We should start to question whether we are being used by technology or whether we are truly using technology. As I have stated many times, I am a big supporter of technology used in the manner it was originally intended. I am not a supporter of technology being used as a means to grab the attention of children, or adults, to push merchandise on them, or as a means to keep children connected to a device while losing connection with real people.

In our effort to "stay at the head of the line," we are too quick to accept marketing advertisements as true research while discounting true research that goes against the advice to buy more devices and programs. Naomi Schaefer Riley points out in her book *Be the Parent, Please* that parents should ask administrators for the actual evidence "that the technology is improving learning outcomes."(Riley,p.126)[36] Administrators are typically given research from the marketing divisions of technology and computer programming companies that was conducted by a research group associated with and paid for by these very companies. Parents should be sure the research they are given is truly independent research.

Remember the chocolate cake. Check the research. If an administrator can produce evidence of positive results, the next question should be, "Who did the research?" Wouldn't you question research done by a company linked to selling a product to the school? True research should be independent and conducted by more than one research team.

Mighty God, thank You for my family. It is my support system in everything I do. Thank You for the unity we have. I pray that You cover us with Your grace so that the devil may not disrupt our peace, for he is roaming around looking for whom he can devour. Help us encourage each other by sharing Your word, which has all Your promises. Pray for each other's strength in moments of weakness. In Jesus Name, Amen.

THE CATCH-22

Schools are always trying to impress parents, school boards, and the community. "Lowell Monke, a professor at Wittenberg University, says he actually thinks most parents are more careful about giving kids technology than professional educators are: 'I was amazed at how much more thoughtlessly schools were willing to adopt this stuff than parents.' Monke believes that this unthinking adoption of technology is "all about schools being scared to death that they are going to get criticized for not having the latest and greatest tools for the kids." (Riley, p.126)[37]

The truth is everyone is trying to impress everyone else. The current, socially accepted thought is that more is better and the latest is the best. No one can look into a student's mind, or into the future, so we are conditioned to make judgment calls based on what is physical and tangible, such as the latest technology, test scores, and the modern features of a school.

We have begun to create schools to look like modern adult workplaces with all the modern features. We are training our youngest preschoolers to be twenty-first-century ready. The decisions makers are thinking about impressing others, whether it is people who voted for them in an election or people in other schools and districts. "Politicians and educators regularly talk about technology as the way to solve educational and income inequality issues in our country. Most schools that cater to low-income children are trying to get them more technology, not less. Schools show parents these shiny new toys as evidence that they are giving their children a leg up, helping to bridge the so-called 'digital divide.' What is more likely is that too much access to technology is actually exacerbating the inequality that already exists."(Riley,p.129)[38]

Frequently, schools are given free access to online learning programs and games for a limited time. Because of the sales pitch and the ease of logging students on, recording their progress, and allowing them to work independently, many administrators are encouraging or even requiring teachers to use these programs. While the success of these programs is usually skewed, students are now playing yet another video game, albeit one labeled "educational." Just like noneducational games, students receive rewards in the form of a banner or ribbon, some type of prize or award to keep them coming back. The company is now hoping to sell this wonderful program to the school system. In many cases, money is not available, and there is no sale. But have no fear—there is another online learning program with a marketing team, waiting for their turn to offer the same promotion. Our students become pawns once again.

While our administrators and educators are assigning these

educational games, our children are quickly learning how to outwit the system. They know how to cheat the game. They know how to bypass the instructional part of the system and go straight for the answers, clicking until they find the correct answer. This is not education. They are playing a game. The skill they are learning is how to bypass the work so they can get to their social media accounts and video games.

The thoughts for what is best for children and their learning have been overshadowed by closed-minded people who think they know more about what is better for children than the actual educators, psychologists, and pediatricians. For children, a stark, modern building is not as important as a secure, warm, welcoming classroom with acceptance for who they are and with the confidence to believe all children are different and learn at different levels. Competition is a game to be played by adults, free of involving children in any way.

YET ANOTHER PROBLEM

America and other countries measure a child's ability and understanding on a standardized test. Doing so is creating even more problems for children. To a great extent, the things that were sold as a way to improve our educational system have in fact done the opposite. Our children are becoming less literate and falling further behind in comparison to other countries and past American generations.

The emphasis on the constant testing of children creates an environment of dislike and dread of reading. Add to that the twenty-first-century technological devices that are being sold as more economical and guaranteed to improve literacy, and the result is the failures we are seeing today.

Children are being deprived of experiencing the enjoyment of reading. In many families and homes, parents snuggle with children to read a book together and enjoy a happy, fictional, make-believe story. This bonding time is being replaced with children propped in front of a device, allowing an inanimate electronic device to read to them. Children are now void of happy memories of crawling in a lap or holding a book together. There are no fond associations with reading at young ages. Parents are so busy that it is easy to let a device replace the time together children need. Parents are being deceived into believing that using a device is just as good or a better alternative than Mom or Dad reading a physical book. The constant barrage of messages is telling parents that computer devices are more important to their children's future than a person reading to them.

The answer is so simple that parents feel it must be wrong. Having confidence, reading together, and sharing books together is about more than the story at hand. It is about happy emotions and fond memories of reading that go far beyond the moment at hand.

When my children were young, we looked forward to going to the library every week for story hour. It was a wonderful time where the children's librarian would share a story, use puppets, and add a multitude of visual aides to her stories. Sometimes she would bring objects for the children or moms to keep. Other times we would pass items around to learn more about the story. At this writing, I cannot remember the title of one book she shared, but I remember this special time. Afterward, my children would use their own library cards to check out their own books to read. Each week, they had multiple worlds to explore. If your public library does not have a story time, I encourage you to campaign for one. As for me, I was able to see how each of my three children responded to a story differently and how they grew to develop their own love for reading. The answer to develop a love of reading is not just one thing. My children did not love to read because we went to story hour once a week. It was because we read to them at home and made books a part of our home. One more little tip: I enrolled each of my children in the book of the month club, and I would do it again today. Although technology offers instant gratification with a download of a book, there is something more special about a package arriving in the mail with a child's name on it. They can hold it and read it over and over, but more important, they know it is especially for them.

Parents must be willing to share in the enjoyment of the book with them and read it to them if necessary. If parents simply throw it aside and do not value it, neither will the child. I am not promising this as a guaranteed formula for good readers or learning to read. It will help children gain an appreciation for books and reading. And it is a much better alternative to what is occurring now in many reading programs.

The second failure I see in the reading programs in American public schools is the use of technology. The reading material is on digital devices for the most part, which can lead to student distractions and lack of focus, as mentioned earlier. It also promotes anxiety because the children know they will be tested on what they are reading. Students then begin spending more time thinking about the test and what will happen if they do not reach a certain score. The focus on the enjoyment of reading is lost. Children are very smart. They understand more about how the system works than the creators and marketers of the tests are willing to accept. A child performing poorly on the reading test will be given tests more frequently in an effort to improve their reading level, whereas a student performing successfully tests less frequently. Do we really think children do not know who the "smart" kids are? And what about the children testing, testing, and testing? Do we really think they enjoy this or that it encourages them to love reading?

The last issue is the trend for reading comprehension tests to be nonfiction. I clearly understand the need to be able to read all classifications of nonfiction, including scientific research, history, instructional manuals, and textbooks. These are all vital in our world. But when students are spending so much time preparing for testing and are not afforded the opportunity to choose and read fiction, I question what we are doing to their imaginations and their ability to visualize characters. They are being deprived of the opportunity to develop their own fond memories of the worlds and places these books can take them. Are we sacrificing a lifelong love for reading for a test score?

According to Michele Borba in her book *UnSelfie; Why Empathetic Kids Succeed in Our All-About-Me World*, "When we read literary fiction, we not only feel "with" the characters, but we also 'do' what they do—and our brains mirror their actions!" In a Michigan State University study, it was revealed that "literary fiction ... not only can make us think deeper, but it also transports us into a different world, helps us feel for the character, and literally lights up our brain!" In addition, Borba states, "The more effort we make trying to figure out a character's intentions, emotions, or thoughts, the greater the odds that our empathy muscles are stretched as well." (Borba, p.80)[39]

WHAT ABOUT LEARNING DURING THE PANDEMIC?

Whenever I discuss learning with technology, this question always comes up: What about learning during the pandemic? Contrary to popular media and social advice, children could learn as well as, if not better, without the internet. You see, our businesses want the extra income, whether it is Internet providers, computer device makers, or software developers. They all love the boost to their bottom line. If you believe they are genuinely interested in the welfare of your children, you are sadly mistaken. "The tech companies do know that the sooner you get kids, adolescents, or teenagers used to your platform, the easier it is to become a lifelong habit. It's no coincidence that Google has made a push into schools with Google Docs, Google Sheets, and the learning management suite Google Classroom."[40]

Many of the Silicon Valley executives send their children to the Waldorf School and other schools that discourage the use of technology until the age of twelve or fourteen. These schools even have some classes outside. They are working on adding additional outside spaces. Although students may need to use technology to some degree, they will remain low-tech as much as possible.[41]

> We do not develop habits of genuine love automatically. We learn by watching effective role models—most specifically by observing how our parents express love for each other day in and day out.
> —Josh McDowell

TAKE CONTROL

Give yourself the power and confidence to make the best decisions for your children. Do not let the whims of society and the trend of the day become your guide. The Bible tells us we are to keep our eyes upon God. It is our job to teach our children and train them in the ways of the Lord. Have the confidence in yourself that our Father in heaven has in you.

> Love the Lord your God with all your heart and with all your soul and with all your strength. These commandments that I give you today are to be upon your hearts. Impress them on your children. Talk about them when you sit at home and when you walk along the road, when you lie down and when you get up. (Deuteronomy 6:5–7 NIV)

TAKEAWAYS

- Parents are cautious about what goes into their bodies and their children's bodies through their mouths, but they are not so cautious about what enters the brain through the eyes.
- Addiction to computer games and programs has been compared to gambling addiction.
- Technology is growing at such a rapid pace that the research about its effects cannot keep up.
- The brain retains more information from a paper book than a digital one.
- Children are missing out on holding a book and being read to by parents.
- Too much use of technology takes away from the human connection children need.
- Children today are lacking empathy for others.

REFERENCES FOR CHAPTER 2

22 S. Kieffer, "How the Brain Works: Johns Hopkins Comprehensive Brain Tumor Center," December 3, 2018, accessed February 14, 2021, https://www.hopkinsmedicine.org/neurology neurosurgery/centers clinics/brain tumor/about-brain-tumors/how-the-brain-works.html.

23 Ibid.

24 N. S. Riley, *Be the Parent, Please* (West Conshohocken PA: Templeton, 2018).

25 Ibid.

26 Ibid.

27 Ibid.

28 Carr, N. G. (2020). *The shallows: What the internet is doing to our brains.* W. W Norton & Company.

29 Ibid.

30 Ibid.

31 Ibid.

32 F. Jabr, "The Reading Brain in the Digital Age: The Science of Paper versus Screens," April 11, 2013, accessed February 2, 2021, https://www.scientificamerican.com/article/reading-paper-screens/.

33 Riley, *Be the Parent, Please.*

34 Ibid.

35 Carr, N.G. (2020). *The Shallows: What the internet is doing to our brains.* W.W. Norton & Company.

36 Riley, *Be the Parent, Please.*

37 Ibid.

38 Ibid.

39 M. Borba, *UnSelfie: Why Empathetic Kids Succeed in Our All-about-Me World* (New York: Touchstone, 2017).

40 C. Weller, "Silicon Valley Parents Are Raising Their Kids Tech-Free—and It Should Be a Red Flag," February 18, 2018, accessed February 16, 2021, https://www.businessinsider.com/silicon-valley-parents-raising-their-kids-tech-free-red-flag-2018-2.

41 E. Einhorn, "Schools Seeking Alternative to Remote Learning Try an Experiment: Outdoor Classrooms," August 10, 2020, accessed February 16, 2021, https://www.nbcnews.com/news/education/tents-yurts-snowsuits-schools-seeking-alternativess-remote-learning-move-classes-n1235809.

CHAPTER 3

Computers, Devices, and Our Children

All a person's ways seem right to him, but the Lord weighs motives. (Proverbs 16:2 CSB)

We are obsessed with our electronic toys. We turn on a device, log into social media, and see into the lives of many people. We click on YouTube and are entertained for hours. Our computers are major tools we use every day at work. We all see the value of technology and the benefits it brings. It is an essential item for scientists developing new drugs and for doctors in the operating room. Let us not forget how important they are to law enforcement and practically every industry in the world. Computers and technology have become essential in our lives. There is no argument there. Technology has improved our lives in so many ways, and future innovations will continue to prove its worth.

However, just because it is good for adults and the adult world does not mean it is good for children.

Unlike the computer and technology industry, which tells us children should be using devices as soon and as much as possible, research has shown that computers are actually harmful to children in many ways.

The calling to be a parent includes the gifts to teach in the ways that are right for you and right for your children. -Robert D. Hales

THE SNAKE OIL WE ARE BUYING

If you are not familiar with the term *snake oil*, its definition according to Merriman-Webster is "something that is sold as medicine but that is not really useful or helpful in any way."[42] While I appreciate the many advances in and advantages of technology, I am aware of the harm it is doing in American schools and to the thinking and learning processes of children.

Children are born with an innate curiosity and motivation to learn. They are eager to discover the world in which they live. This curiosity is a natural gift from God to explore the world around them. Anyone who has ever been around babies knows the joy and happiness they experience when they first discover their hands and feet. And when they discover they can control these little hands and feet, they are mesmerized by this simple revelation. Then when they discover how to move, whether it is by crawling, scooting, or walking, they spend countless hours discovering all the objects within their reach. This is a magical time in their lives. Be careful not to limit this mental growing experience by placing a device in front of them to watch. God created a wonderful world for our children to explore. This is an especially important time in developmental learning and the development of a baby's mind.

Consequently, God has given children boundaries when they are born. They are unable to roll over at first. Then when they can roll over, they are unable to sit up unassisted. Gradually, as they grow, they are figuring things out and storing this information in their brains. God has created a natural pattern of growing and learning for each person. Each week or month brings a new stage of development and discovery. Growing into a healthy child is the ability to figure things out and gradually test limits. Of course, this continues throughout life as they grow and encounter more of the world.

Mister Rogers was an advocate for the emotional and mental health of happy, secure children. He spent his career working with children and psychologists to ensure all his shows and books were geared around the healthy development of children. In his book *Mister Rogers Talks with Parents*, he quotes an article from the March 1979 issue of *Psychology Today*:

> Our research on imaginative play in early childhood suggests that private fantasy has significant benefits for a growing child. Children of three or four who engage in pretending or make-believe play not only appear to be happier, but also are more fluent verbally and show more cooperation and sharing behavior. They can wait quietly or delay gratification, can concentrate better and seem to be more empathic and less aggressive, thanks to their use of private fantasy. (Rogers, p.111)[43]

I am a big advocate of parents sitting down with their children to watch Mister Rogers—and to watch it with the eyes of a child. If you do not already know, Mister Rogers teaches children how to use make-believe to deal with those situations that may be beyond their control. Rather than putting a device in front of children, encourage them to make-believe. They can use their imaginations to make-believe they are anything or anybody they want to be. Children using make-believe are using very sophisticated mental processes. For example, if they are pretending to be a doctor, their thought processes involve how a doctor dresses, what instruments they use, how they talk to a patient, what their office looks like, and much more. As you can see, this is much more thought than goes into a passive activity of watching a video or pressing buttons.

In this world of make-believe, they are mentally processing and building from their personal experience, their memories, the things they have seen in a book or on TV, and even the way they imagine it to be. They are solving extremely complicated mental problems. And as Mister Rogers points out, all these things add up to being happier, being more verbally fluent, being cooperative, and being more empathic toward others. No computer device can replace the human element of learning we all need, especially children who are just beginning to learn about this wonderful world.

The point is our world has changed and continues to change, which includes great technological advances. Our world has now evolved into most of society with the attitude "Me first, and too bad for anyone else." Our children are no longer emphatic about the needs of others but are selfish and self-centered, grabbing all they can for themselves. Even well-meaning parents are encouraging this thought process. This is not a statement of blame or criticism but of the changes in society that have led to this shift. There are many influences that fronted this, including the popularity of reality television shows that portray life as winning, the focus on social media that encourages profiting from superficial, and shallow tasks with little to no concentration. Add to that the pressure from marketing and media for our children to not only excel but to become the best, thereby becoming the most profitable in life.

We are victims of a greedy world. Of course, we want the best for our families and our children. We love them. We are fed a steady diet of messages from media and marketing companies telling us exactly what we need to do to prove this love. We do not want to mess up. We only have one chance to raise our children, so we cannot let a moment pass that we are not fighting the fight for our children. Unfortunately, much of this philosophy is opposite of what the Bible teaches. We are taught in the Bible to humble ourselves. This concept is not only against modern culture but also difficult to live by in our daily lives. The Bible tells us in Philippians 2:3–4 (NIV), "Do nothing out of selfish ambition or vain conceit, but in humility consider others better than yourselves. Each of you should look not only to your own interests, but also to the interests of others."

CAUTION TO PARENTS

One of the most concerning things to come out of our obsession with Facebook and the need to constantly monitor the lives of others is the continuous barrage of fake happy lives, perfect families, and perfect children. I understand parents are proud of their children; I am proud of my children too. But we should stop to consider the messages we are sending them when we are posting about our "perfect" families.

In the past decade, parents (especially moms and grandparents) post their children's every little accomplishment. I know we are happy and want to share this joy. But there are three things we should consider first.

1. What message does this send our children? They know we are proud of them for their wins and their high scores. But many children will feel they are a disappointment when they no longer win or when their grades drop. No one can ride on the high clouds forever. There will come a time when failures and disappointments happen. Children need to have confidence they will be loved just as much when this occurs as when they are successful.

2. Think about a family with more than one child. What if sports or education comes easy to one child but is difficult to another child? How do you think the struggling child feels? What kind of impact will this leave if praise is heaped upon one child and not the other? Some parents may think this type of behavior will inspire the low performing child, but in actuality it causes them to be resentful and withdrawn from the family.

3. Do your friends care if your children have high grades or win trophies? Whom are we trying to impress? It reminds me of an old *I Love Lucy* episode where Lucy and Ricky keep showing videos of Little Ricky to Fred and Ethel. Fred and Ethel love Little Ricky but are absolutely tired of seeing every accomplishment, small or large. They are bored to death. Be

careful not to be those parents for the sake of your children and your friends.

What has not changed over time is how we all develop mentally. Children are still born the same way. They still grow the same way physically, and they still have the same needs in order to be emotionally happy and secure. However, with the encouragement of tech companies, we buy into their sales pitches and ignore the common sense and advice of past generations.

Mister Rogers's wisdom continues to prevail: "I have no doubt that millions of children of all ages are getting an overdose of mechanical entertainment and suffering a deficiency in healthier forms of *play*. Although I do not know what the consequences will be, I feel sure they will be measurable and specific and will affect the quality of human relationships and an individual's capacity for self-development." (Rogers, p.121)[44]

What we have failed to recognize and address is that children in past generations were happier, more motivated, and more empathic toward others. Even with new technology and new devices, our hearts are still the driving force of our commitments to the things we hold dear and cherish. It is not the money one acquires that makes them happy but the love of God, family, and others.

The book of Proverbs outlines how to find happiness.

The fear of the Lord is the beginning of knowledge; fools despise wisdom and discipline. (Proverbs 1:7 CSB)

The inexperienced one believes anything, but the sensible one watches his steps. (Proverbs 14:15 CSB)

The one who understands a matter finds success, and the one who trusts in the Lord will be happy. (Proverbs 16:20 CSB)

I encourage people to search their hearts and to pray for guidance from God on the path He has for your children. Understand that the path will not always be easy, but in the end God's glory will be worth it all. It is hard to let go of the control, but God has plans for all of us—better plans than we could ever imagine. God's plans for us are not for our glory but for His glory.

> Parents, you will teach your children more by scheduling regular times to nurture the relationship between husband and wife than you would ever teach them through a lecture on commitment. Although it is important for you pray to for your child, seeking the Lord for that perfect spouse for them, it is equally important that you teach them through your example how to cherish the future gift of a companion that the Lord has in store for them.
> —Katherine Walden

WHAT ABOUT CHILDREN OF SILICON VALLEY EXECUTIVES?

I have already described the schools the children of Silicon Valley attend and the schools of the politicians who are making the decisions for our children. We are quick to do what they tell us, but we are slow to question why they choose a different route for their children.

WALDORF SCHOOL ATTENDED BY MANY CHILDREN OF SILICON VALLEY EXECUTIVES

Unlike the public schools in the United States, Waldorf School does not adhere to standardized testing or to the use of computers for students until the age of fourteen.

A day for kindergarten students includes plenty of playtime, cooking, story time, snack, nap, afternoon play, and language arts circle.

There is no pressure for testing or drilling from the teachers. Instead, it is based around the natural curiosity and discovery of the children.

By seventh grade, language arts classes are focused on a classic novel and the use of book reports. The lesson includes vocabulary, writing, comprehension, and questions. A seventh-grade math lesson focuses on a long-term study of the Fibonacci series, with problems centered around the concept. There are no disconnected concepts or random lessons. There is only one concept for students to focus on at a time in order to gain greater understanding through using a variety of tools to solve problems.

Throughout the year, children have an extremely limited number of concepts, each developed with great understanding. There is no concern about using technology to tackle problems. The philosophy of the school is that technology can wait until children are intellectually ready.[45]

> These anti-technology schools have found popularity in an unlikely place: Silicon Valley. Parents who work in high-tech industries find them particularly appealing. Back-to-school nights at Waldorf schools are a who is who of the technology world, with executives from eBay, Google, Yahoo, Apple, and Hewlett-Packard who all choose to send their kids to such schools. Seventy-five percent of Waldorf students in Silicon Valley have ties to the tech industry ... As Alan Eagle, an executive at Google who is a Waldorf parent and has a computer science degree from Dartmouth, explains, "At Google and all these places, we make technology as brain-dead easy to use as possible. There's no reason why kids can't figure it out when they get older." (Clement, Miles p.175)[46]

Research is proving the tech parents are correct in limiting technology for their children. "An actual peer-reviewed study by Duke University economist Jacob Vigdor and his team shows that computer technology is associated with 'statistically significant and persistently negative impacts on student math and reading test scores.'"[47]

OBSTACLES WHEN YOU TRY TO SWIM AGAINST THE CURRENT

There are parents and teachers who recognize the downfall of technology. They are concerned about the influence of technology on the lives of their children and family but feel compelled to continue on the current path of our school and social culture. It has become exceedingly difficult for parents and teachers who feel this is not the best way to educate children for different reasons. Peer pressure, along with the constant messages and images in the media of children working on computers, makes it exceedingly difficult. It takes a great deal of confidence and support to be different, even when you know you are right. Hang in there! We hope help is on the way!

The following is a prayer for middle and high school students.

> Lord Jesus,
> I dedicate my studies to You. Give me the knowledge and skills in all subjects. Grant me the grace to understand what is taught in class. Help me to be hardworking and not lazy in class and in extracurricular activities. Lord, thank You for the gifts and talents that you have given me. May I use them to learn and further my spiritual life. Lord, help me to follow the path You have laid for me. Reveal Your love and plans to me in everything that I learn. In Jesus's name I pray, amen.

THROUGH THE EYES OF PARENTS WANTING TO GO TECH-FREE

When the designers and developers of computer and internet programs are leery and even restrictive about the use of these programs for their own children, it should be a reason for all of us to give pause and contemplate the exposure of these programs on our children. But American parents are up against more difficult obstacles. The typical American parent is not a celebrity or a Silicon Valley executive, making it even more difficult to choose an anti-technology lifestyle for their children.

The executives and high influential people of Silicon Valley choosing the anti-technology route already consider themselves elite. They are paying for expensive private schools. These parents are not concerned about being labeled as different—they embrace it. We need to follow this example and change our mindset too. After all, our children can be the "new elite" in public schools.

Please consider the following.

1. The schools are encouraging the use of computers and devices for children, promising it is the only way to stay ahead in the future.
2. Most assigned books and textbooks are available only online. Many homework assignments are to be completed online.
3. Opting out of technology will almost certainly make it harder for children in the short term. Teachers who encourage the use of technology will not be happy with the extra work needed for the child who has parents requesting less technology. Children who are different for any reason are usually treated as an outcast or outsider by their peers.
4. Friends and family may add pressure. Well-meaning friends and family stress how their children are using the technology and excelling. Some go so far as to imply withholding technology is cruel to children.

THROUGH THE EYES OF TEACHERS SEEING THE DISADVANTAGES OF TECH

Some teachers do not want to use technology consistently. Consider their point of view.

1. There are many teachers who have experienced the failures of technology in their classrooms. Many of these teachers are eager to make changes but do not have the authority to do so.

2. Teachers in many states are evaluated based on observations from administrators and on student test scores. The observations include how technology is being used by both students and teachers for learning. Any teacher refusing to use technology, or who does not have their students constantly tuned in, are at risk of a poor rating on their evaluations, leading to action plans and job loss.

3. American education in today's world is also about pleasing parents. In almost all schools, there are a few demanding parents who are active and involved in the school. Many people do not know that these parents seem to always be present in the school. Although it is a good idea to volunteer in your child's school, there are some helicopter parents who enjoy "hanging out" at school. These parents are valuable because they are available to assist with programs and can assist teachers with class preparation and organization.. Administrators are like proud parents: they want to brag on their school and list reasons why their school is the best. They want to impress parents and the community. Administrators understand happy parents report great things to friends online and in the community. While unhappy parents do the same, they often express their disappointments about the administration and teachers to anyone willing to listen.

4. The superintendent and school board have a budget and need to spend money on the things that will impress the community. School systems rely on funding from city and county boards to balance budgets.

5. Education is political in America. The pressure is on the superintendent to keep pushing students. After all, no one wants to go to the school at the low end of the testing spectrum.

6. The school system has poured a lot of money into more bandwidth, computers, and educational programs. People are expecting to see the wonderful results that were promised. Teachers are instructed and expected to move into technology full force. It is not an option.

There is a fine line between healthy parental love and child worship. We know the latter has happened when we begin compromising God's will for the sake of our children or their activities ... Compromise always points to idolatry. It displeases God. He does not like competitors, especially when they are our children.
—William Farley, *Gospel-Powered Parenting* (Phillipsburg, NJ: P&R, 2009), 33

WHO ARE THE PROPONENTS OF COMPUTER DEVICES IN EDUCATION? THROUGH THE EYES OF SOCIETY

1. Most people view the Internet and technology as the way of the future. Anyone refusing to recognize this is not living in the real world.

2. Schools are promoting technology; the children are doing PowerPoints and research online. It is so much better than previous generations. How could anything be wrong?

3. Everyone except for a few "old people" are using smartphones, computers, and devices all day. All of these people cannot be wrong. The person not onboard has to be wrong.

4. Technology is wonderful! It occupies the family, and everyone is happy. Parents know their children are home connecting with friends online. It makes traveling in the car so much easier!

5. Children are now happy to stay at home. All parents need to do is buy the latest technology devices or video games. Children are not being harmed if they are in their rooms.

THROUGH THE EYES OF POLITICIANS AND SILICON VALLEY EXECUTIVES

1. Our economy is driven by big business. The companies making technology devices employ a lot of people all over the world. A lot of people depend on the success of these companies to drive the economy.
2. The US education system spends millions (possibly billions) of dollars in equipping the classrooms with the latest technology devices. Jobs would be lost, and the economy would suffer without the education dollars in technology.
3. Profits are important to the health of the technology companies. It is important to keep schools connected online in order to drive those profits. Taxpayers are paying for devices and technology, which in turn is driving the economy and employment numbers.
4. There is a trickle-down effect of using technology in all grades. Children must be exposed to the devices. Add them to their birthday and Christmas lists. Parents want nothing more than to make their children happy.

The family should be a closely knit group. The home should be a self-contained shelter of security; a kind of school where life's basic lessons are taught; and a kind of church where God is honored; a place where wholesome recreation and simple pleasures are enjoyed.
—Billy Graham

WARNING TO PARENTS

> There is a way that seems right to a man, but in the end,
> it leads to death. (Proverbs 14:12 NIV)

As a general rule, technology is not bad or harmful to adults. It is imperative parents understand what is appropriate for children and what is not.

Parents should do their own research. No one gives a child a car without knowing something about it. We do not assume that just because we drive a car, our children should have one too. Nor do we assume that because our neighbor gave their child a car at fifteen years old, we should give our child a car at thirteen years old. This may seem like an exaggeration, but there are parents who would allow children to drive at much younger ages were it not for laws prohibiting it.

Unfortunately for our children, the Internet and technology are so new that the laws about health and safety for children have not yet been created. Consider taking time to research first what your children are doing with technology. The mental and emotional health of our children is too valuable to risk.

TAKEAWAYS

- There are things, including many technological devices, that may be appropriate for adults but are not meant for children.
- Americans and other countries believe technology and electronic devices are the way of the future.
- Children are born with a natural curiosity about the world in which they live. Technology is not needed for them to explore this world.
- Mr. Rogers understood decades ago that children were headed for an unhealthy, electronic overload.
- Many economies are now dependent on the dollars generated by the use of technologies in the public schools.

- Even when parents and teachers want to unplug their children from technology, schools and society make it almost impossible.
- Silicon Valley executives have recognized the harm of technology at an early age. Most send their children to nontechnology schools.
- Technology is a good thing when used by adults and older children for appropriate reasons.

REFERENCES FOR CHAPTER 3

42 "Snake Oil," accessed November 20, 2020, https://www.merriam-webster.com/dictionary/snake oil.

43 F. Rogers and B. Head, *Mister Rogers Talks with Parents* (New York: Barnes & Noble, 1994).

44 Ibid.

45 "The Waldorf Difference" accessed November 21, 2020, https://www.gmws.org/the-waldorf-difference.

46 J. Clement and M. Miles, *Screen Schooled: Two Veteran Teachers Expose How Technology Overuse Is Making Our Kids Dumber* (Melbourne: Black, 2018).

47 Ibid.

CHAPTER 4

American Schools Are Doing It Wrong

Finland has been one of the top countries in successful education for the past two decades. Their system is polar opposite to the United States, yet they are producing much better results. This is based on a standardized test, Programme for International Student Assessment (PISA), given to fifteen-year-olds in more than forty countries around the world. According to the first PISA results in 2000, Finland ranked the highest in the world in reading comprehension. In 2003, Finland led in math. Three years later, in 2006, they were first in science. Then in 2009, Finland was "second in science, third in reading and sixth in math."[48] All these subjects continue to be well above the United States, with scores consistently in the middle.[49] Yet the US educational administration refuses to take notice, make changes in a failing system, or recognize the importance of the work going on in Finland.

> The fear of the Lord is the beginning of knowledge, but fools despise wisdom and discipline. (Proverbs 1:7 NIV)

> Lord, we put our children who are in high school into Your hands. There is so much we can do as parents, but ultimately You are the one who knows their end from the beginning. May our children not set their eyes and mind on things that do not glorify Your name

while at school. Let no harm befall them, dear Lord. Be their source of encouragement, especially when things at school become difficult. Grant them grace to excel in everything they do, and may they never be ashamed of the gospel of Jesus Christ when they are interacting with their peers. Lord, connect them to good friends who will impact their faith positively for the glory of Your name. In Jesus's name I pray, amen.

In looking at Finland and their school system, I examined not only the test scores but also the way children were treated. In digging deeper, we find sound reasons for the improvement in the education in Finland by examining how children are treated and the amount of stress placed on children. Finland encourages children to be children; they promote children learning through play and advocate teaching children to aspire to be givers and not takers. Children in Finland are urged to learn to contribute to better the community and humanity.

Education is not just about test scores or the amount of money a country spends. Education is about working with the whole child. It is understanding children are more than numbers. Children need an environment where they are accepted for who they are; they need an environment that allows them to be a square peg in the round hole. Children need love along with understanding, acceptance, and a nurturing environment. Children are living, breathing human beings created by God. They are not objects to be used as guinea pigs. They should not be tested like lab mice in order to record data and make comparisons.

In the United States and many other countries that emphasize data, there are many nurturing, caring, loving people. We are not disputing that in any way. However, when data and top scores are the most important factors, it makes it almost impossible for these wonderful, dedicated teachers to spend time where it is really needed: in the growth and development of the character and security of the children so they can become independent thinkers and risk takers.

The Bible tells us we are each created as individuals.

I chose you before I formed you in the womb; I set you
apart before you were born. I appointed you a prophet
to the nations. (Jeremiah 1:5 CSB)

God had a plan for us and our children before we were born. God,
who loves us and cares for us, has already decided our path and the path
of our children. The easy path is to go along with everyone else, but
God's path will take us in a different direction with a much different
purpose.

The illiterate of the 21st century will not be those who
cannot read and write, but those who cannot learn,
unlearn, and relearn.
—Alvin Toffler

WHY IGNORE THIS DATA?

Perhaps one of the reasons the United States refuses to get off a
path leading to continued failure and increased mental health issues in
children is due to the huge investment in money and resources already
in place. We have discovered much of this money spent on education
in the United States goes to big corporations in the tech and testing
industries. Lobbyists keep lawmakers abreast of the latest rhetoric from
these industries, promising that more advanced educational gains are
just on the horizon.

In 2016, the United States spent $12,184 per student through
primary grades, and Finland spent $9,477. The average cost of world
countries according to the Organization for Economic Cooperation and
Development (OECD) was $8,470. In secondary grades, the United
States spent $13,845 as Finland spent $10,472, and the OECD reported
$9,968 per student.[50]

The US education system is run by politicians with a huge influence
from testing corporations and technology industries. But possibly the
biggest reason the United States fails to make changes is that the

government refuses to relinquish control of the education system to the educators and teachers. These professionals are much more qualified to make decisions about education than the politicians who have little to no experience working with children. This causes one to wonder whether the driving force for politicians is more about bragging rights and who will get the credit if test scores do improve. If politicians are focused on the next election or their legacy, it would stand to reason that they need concrete evidence of their accomplishments. Hence, the children are necessary to drive these accomplishments, even if they fail. In the meantime, what is happening to these children and their confidence, their reasoning abilities, their sense of community, and their desire to contribute to humanitarian efforts?

FINNISH VS. US EDUCATION SYSTEMS

Let us look at the first important difference to note about the Finnish school systems: its focus on the whole child. Unlike the American system, this emphasis is not on preparing students to enter the adult world. The Finnish understand the mental, social, and emotional development of children and are completely committed to implementing the requirements to nourish the child. "Their stated goal for basic education is 'to support pupils' growth toward humanity and ethically responsible membership of society and to provide them with the knowledge and skills needed in life."[51] While the United States focuses on competitiveness and being at the top, Finland sees a bigger picture. Finland encourages and promotes students to be ethically responsible to "support growth toward humanity," as a part of the and skills needed for life.

As the United States continues to ignore the importance of the whole child (including mental health), the numbers of young people with depression and suicidal tendencies continues to grow at alarming rates. US public schools isolate mental health into a single class taught by a licensed school counselor in elementary school. Sometimes these classes are once a week, but more often they are once or twice per month. Mental health is not an issue that can be taught as a class. Mental health is the result of nurturing and supporting the emotional needs of children as they grow and develop. It is about recognizing that children are not mini adults and should not be rushed into the adulthood.

By the time children reach middle school (twelve to thirteen years old), there is no longer time or resources available for counseling. There are exceptions. If a student needs counseling, the counselor is available a few days a week by appointment. In high school, counselors are available only by appointment. These are usually offered first to seniors preparing for college entrance.

In the classroom, daily schedules are regulated to teaching the tested subjects in isolation of each other. This is especially true in third through fifth grade. Students are on a very rigid schedule, not allowing time for teachers to personally connect with students. Teachers are under pressure to have students show mastery in specific concepts through benchmark tests throughout the year. Time and emphasis are not on the whole child that could improve the mental, social, and emotional well-being of children.

I do not mean to sound pessimistic, and I recognize there are many caring people in US schools, as well as many wonderful educators. These individuals devote a lifetime to working with children. Many take home with them not only their work but also the problems of their students. This chapter is no reflection of these people. I dare say most people who go into education in the United States do so with the aim to help children and make the world a better place. My fear is that most Americans are unaware of the pressure put on children and of more successful ways to educate our children.

As stated earlier, the PISA compares students of the same age all around the world. Although Finland may move up and down a few slots on the ranking, it consistently stays well above the United States and continually ranks in the top ten.[52] Maybe it is time parents were made aware of what Finland is doing and of what the United States fails to do.

To be fair, there are many charter public schools in the United States. These schools are afforded the luxury of altering their curriculum somewhat. There are also many science, technology, engineering, and math (STEM) programs doing an outstanding job of encouraging creativity, innovation, and learning. Unfortunately, these are not the norm, and are unavailable to every student. Many of the STEM activities are developed to help in a humanitarian way, but there is often competition to win.

The Bible teaches us to do good for the sake of helping others, not for any reward. In Matthew we are instructed,

> Be careful not to do your acts of righteousness before men, to be seen by them. If you do, you will have no reward from your Father in heaven. So, when you give to the needy, do not announce it with trumpets, as the hypocrites do in the synagogues and on the streets, to be honored by men. I tell you the truth, they have received their reward in full. But when you give to the needy, do not let your left hand know what your right hand is doing, so that your giving may be in secret. Then your Father, who sees what is done in secret, will reward you. (Matthew 6:14 NIV)

Below are some strategies Finland implements that allow it to continue to rank high in the world.

1. Education is not treated as a business corporation "where tough competition, measurement-based accountability and performance-determined pay are common principles. Instead, Finland's successful education systems rely on collaboration, trust, and collegial responsibility in and between schools."[53]
2. There is a high regard for the teaching profession. Teachers are treated as professionals and are trusted to make decisions about education. They are required to have a master's degree and participate in continuing education that involves "advanced academic education, solid scientific and practical knowledge, and continuous on-the-job training."[54]

3. Emphasis is placed on the whole child, which includes "equity of education outcomes, well-being, and arts, music, drama and physical education." Students are not judged by test scores, and the Finnish understand that the well-being of a child involves more than just math and reading.

4. The instructional curriculum is developed by the teachers and education providers. Schools have more flexibility in the design of the curriculum and the supervision of how it is delivered and designed. There is a national core curriculum for basic education that is considered an extremely basic guide for education and instruction.

5. It is acceptable for schools to have different theoretical and administrative views and educational designs in achieving successful student education. Individual schools and authorities are trusted to devise plans for the betterment of the students they teach.

6. Schools are not judged on any scores. Everyone is working toward the best education for the whole child, which is geared to the children they teach and each student's individual needs.

The NCC (National Core Curriculum), Finland's guide for education and instruction, states that the specific aim at the school level is that children would:

- Understand the relationship and interdependencies between different learning contents.
- Be able to combine the knowledge and skills learned in different disciplines to form meaningful wholes.
- Be able to apply knowledge and use it in collaborative learning settings.[55]

To be successful citizens, which is the ultimate goal for every country's students, the core goal must be for each student to make connections with each other and the world around them. Each must be willing to work both independently and as a team for the betterment of the community, society, and economy.

The greatest differences between the United States' and Finland's approach to education is Finland's

- trust in teachers,
- collaboration among schools, and
- visionary leadership.[56]

DIFFERENCES THAT HAVE LED TO BETTER STUDENT PERFORMANCE

In an article in the *World Economic Forum* by Abby Jackson, entitled *"Finland Has One of the World's Best Education Systems,"* Jackson points out even more differences. The sad reality is most of these differences do not cost anything but produce much better results. In the United States, money is spent on one new program after another, year after year, with no positive results. Some programs prove only to be a waste of time and money.

FINLAND'S EDUCATION

Only one standardized test, the national matriculation examination, is given to students. They are assessed at the end of secondary school.[57] The test consists of thought-provoking questions and is graded by teachers. One example of a question is, "In what sense are happiness, good life and well-being ethical concepts?" Other topics ask students "to show their ability to cope with issues related to evolution, losing a job, dieting, political issues, violence, war, ethics in sports, junk food, sex, drugs, and popular music. These issues span across subject areas and require multi-disciplinary knowledge and skills."[58] This ability to draw on communication and comprehension skills to debate a point, share knowledge, provide examples, and most important describe the mental and social understanding of the topics are critical to becoming well-rounded contributing members of society.

US EDUCATION

Standardized tests are given every year beginning in third grade over a period of multiple hours and multiple days at the end of the school year. There are standardized benchmarks given in reading and math, with testing beginning as early as kindergarten. These are given at the end of the reporting period. The tests are multiple choice, with no written portions to view student comprehension of the subject. Each subject is tested independently of the others. Teachers do not grade the tests; computers and scanners grade and assess each student. Students and teachers are informed multiple times throughout the year about the importance of the scores on these tests, meaning low scores could require summer school or retention for students and job loss for teachers. Both students and teachers live in dread, anxiety, and fear of testing.

FINLAND'S EDUCATION

Play is essential to student success. The Finnish education system understands the research supporting this and adheres to the philosophy that children learn through play. Children are expected to play, release energy, and enjoy social interactions. Students are given only 2.8 hours of homework per week (about thirty minutes per night) on average. By law, students are required to take fifteen-minute breaks for every forty-five minutes of instruction.[59]

US EDUCATION

Students generally have thirty to forty-five minutes of recess a day, but only in elementary school. Many schools and teachers adhere to this only because this required recess has become law in many states. By middle school, students may have a class in physical education, lasting forty-five to ninety minutes, but some semesters have no physical education. Again, this only happens in some schools because it is state law. Homework, on average, is six hours per week (about 1.25 hours each night). Little time is allotted for socialization and free play at school.

Most school systems require teachers to teach subjects independently of each other for a specific amount of time during the school day. For example, the following page displays a schedule that is typical for elementary third through fifth graders.

Daily Schedule

- 7:30–8:00: Morning Work (usually practice in math)
- 8:00–9:30: English/Language Arts (includes reading aloud, reading groups, comprehension, writing, phonics, spelling, and language)
- 9:30–10:30: Math (includes basic skills practice, main lesson, practice in the new skill, word problem practice)
- 10:30–11:00: Recess (includes travel time to and from the playground, with an average of fifteen to twenty minutes usually occurring)
- 11:00–12:00: Science
- 12:00–12:30: Lunch. Many schools require five to ten minutes of eating prior to socializing, sometimes leaving less than ten minutes for student socialization. Many teachers also require assigned seating.
- 12:30–1:15: Special Classes (PE, art, media, computer, guidance, music). These classes meet one assigned day per week.
- 1:15–1:45: Independent Reading. Schools approach this time in different ways. It may be DEAR (Drop Everything and Read), accelerated reading (reading a book and taking a multiple-choice test), or independent reading with teacher conferencing with individual students. This may be a time for struggling readers to get more attention, but above average or gifted students tend to not receive more attention)

- 1:45–2:30: Social Studies. Many times, this is treated as another time slot for student practice in reading short passages and answering multiple choice questions.
- 2:30: Dismissed

Not every classroom schedule is this way. In schools that emphasize testing and scores, this is a typical day. There are even school systems that require teachers to use the exact same lessons for each subject so that administrators may go into any fourth-grade classroom during math and see the exact same lesson being taught exactly the same way. Teachers not adhering to the schedule (posted in the room and submitted to the administration) or at the same pace as colleagues are at risk of being reprimanded, with this documentation noted on the teacher's evaluation forms.

FINNISH EDUCATION

College is free, which includes a bachelor's degree, master's degree, and even a doctoral degree. All college tuition is free in Finland.[60]

US EDUCATION

College in the United States is awfully expensive. Costs in 2020 range from an average of $9,687 for public college, and in-state tuition costs are $35,087 for private colleges. Ivy League colleges such as Harvard or Yale could be up to $60,000. Students have additional costs such as school fees, room and board, textbooks and supplies, and lab materials.[61]

Student loans have been used to make college possible for many. These loans have also caused many to leave college with tens of thousands of dollars in debt and no guarantee to find a job in their field.

FINLAND'S EDUCATION

"Teaching is one of the most revered professions with a relatively high barrier to entry."[62] Teachers on every level are respected and revered by parents and students alike.

US EDUCATION

Schools are driven by money that may or may not be granted for budgets due to testing scores, industries with their own agendas, parents, school boards, Parent Teacher Associations, and government agencies (state, county, and city commissioners) weighing in on the system. The system has become a balancing act of keeping everyone happy in order to get support. The well-being of children is decided by boards, not educators. Respect for educators has been lost by the drive to allow parents to make changes when they disagree with decisions made by teachers. School boards determine, through the recommendation from the superintendents, how to invest the resources and how to ensure teachers adhere to new programs.

The individual needs of the child have been lost. Many times, expensive programs are introduced as the latest and greatest for increasing student test scores. These tend to have fallible research provided by the industry promoting the program. As discussed earlier, this is skewed research. After administrators and educators participate in required weekly training occurring for hours after the school day, complete required extensive extra documentation on students that the new program sets in place, receive and perform impromptu observations to ensure said program is correctly administered, and attend additional meetings to compare notes, observations, and documentation in order to provide feedback to administration. The new program may last two years only to be dropped as soon as the promised elevation in test scores does not happen. With the drive for increased test scores, a new, "improved" program that is just as expensive (or in many cases more expensive) as the first program is adapted, and the cycle continues.

FOR THE SKEPTICS

There will be some who argue that the United States has too many obstacles to overcome, such as lower socioeconomic students, English language learners, or students living in drug-infested neighborhoods. While I would never underestimate the severity of these problems, there are ways our education system could begin making changes that would render a positive impact many of these students. An article in the *Smithsonian* Magazine by LynNell Hancock entitled "Why Are Finland's Schools Successful?" addresses some of these issues.

> Many schools are small enough so that teachers know every student. If one method fails, teachers consult with colleagues to try something else. They seem to relish the challenges. Nearly 30 percent of Finland's children receive some kind of special help during their first nine years of school ... in one school of 240 first nine years of school, more than half of its 150 elementary level students are immigrants--from Somalia, Iraq, Russia, Bangladesh, Estonia, and Ethiopia, among other nations.[63]

> In the United States, which has muddled along in the middle for the past decade, government officials have attempted to introduce marketplace competition into public schools. In recent years, a group of Wall Street financiers and philanthropists such as Bill Gates have put money behind private-sector ideas, such as vouchers, data-driven curriculum and charter schools, which have doubled in number in the past decade. President Obama too, has apparently bet on competition. His Race to the Top initiative invites states to compete for federal dollars using tests and other methods to measure teachers, a philosophy that would not fly in Finland. "I think, in fact, teachers would tear off their shirts," said

Timo Heikkinen, a Helsinki Principal with 24 years of teaching experience. "If you only measure the statistics, you miss the human aspect ... Americans like all these bars and graphs and colored charts. It is nonsense. We know much more about the children than these tests can tell us," reports veteran teacher Kari Louhivuori.[64]

Unlike the United States, Finland goes low-tech. There is limited technology even available to students. "In math class, the teacher shuts off the Smartboard and begins drafting perfect circles on a chalkboard. The students—some of the highest-achieving in the world—cut up graphing paper while solving equations using their clunky plastic calculator. Finnish students and teachers did not need laptops and iPads to get to the top of international rankings, said Krista Kiuru, Minister of Education and Science at the Finnish Parliament. And officials say they aren't interest in using them to stay there."[65]

Unlike the United States, who has spent billions of dollars on technology and constant standardized testing, Finland's philosophy has been proven repeatedly to work and produce positive results, and it continues to improve the lives of the people. "The Nordic country uses innovative teaching strategies in the classroom, just generally without incorporating technology. Private schools and charter schools are not part of the mix, and all education is essentially free. Powerful teachers' unions work hand in hand with the government, which went to great lengths to revamp teacher training. The profession is revered and respected, and government has no bearing on assessing a teacher's performance in the classroom."[66]

Finally, one of the most important differences between Finland and the United States is the view of competition. In the United States, everything from grades to sports, electronic devices, and where we live is about competing. Americans want to be first. Americans want the best. Most Americans like to brag and boast about themselves and their families. This is perhaps the difference I find most outrageous about many America's way of life compared to the way of life in Finland.

In contrast, the Finnish "culture is about bettering oneself instead of beating other nations."[67]

Throughout the book of Proverbs, we read about the importance of wisdom. Studying and applying ourselves is very commendable.

> The heart of the discerning acquires knowledge; the ears of the wise seek it out. (Proverbs 18:15 NIV)

The Bible clearly teaches us to seek knowledge and wisdom. It also teaches us to love and care for each other and to put others before ourselves. This is where the culture in the United States is failing.

> He who gives to the poor will lack nothing, but he who closes his eyes to them receives many curses. (Proverb 28:27 NIV)

> How much better to get wisdom than gold, to choose understanding rather than silver! (Proverbs 16:16 NIV)

> If anyone has material possessions and sees his brother in need but has no pity on him, how can the love of God be in him? Dear Children, let us not love with words or tongue but with actions and in truth. (1 John 3:17–18 NIV)

We have become a selfish culture, interested only in our material possessions and being first at everything. Clearly we are not first in developing our most precious resource—our children.

Education should never be measured by the price of its toys (technology) or by tests given over a few days at the end of the year.

Education occurs naturally and constantly with children. It is called *childhood*. Children should be allowed to be children! They are not mini adults. They will have many years to be adults in the adult world, with adult problems. Please do not rush them. Children all over the world are being exposed to adult material and adult stress at earlier ages. Let them live the life of a child and be innocent for as long as possible. There will be plenty time for the adult world and the problems that come with it later.

> Defend the weak and the fatherless; uphold the cause
> of the poor and the oppressed. Rescue the weak and
> the needy; deliver them from the hand of the wicked.
> (Psalm 82:3–4 NIV)

TAKEAWAYS

- Children in the United States are under more pressure to produce high test scores.
- Finland ranks at the top ten countries in the world for education.
- The United States has very rigid school schedule for students.
- Finland requires fifteen-minute breaks after every forty-five minutes of instruction.
- The United States assigns an average of six hours of homework every week.
- Finland assigns an average of 2.8 hours of homework every week.
- The education system in Finland focuses on the whole child.
- The United States focuses on reading and math throughout school, while adding other subjects in later grades.

REFERENCES FOR CHAPTER 4

48 L. Hancock, "Why Are Finland's Schools Successful?" September 1, 2011, accessed December 02, 2020, https://www.smithsonianmag.com/innovation/why-are-finlands-schools-successful-49859555/.
49 Ibid.
50 "Finland: Governance and Accountability," September 30, 2019, accessed February 11, 2021, https://ncee.org/what-we-do/center-on-international-education-benchmarking/top-performing-countries/finland-overview/finland-system-and-school-organization/.

51 Kevin Dickinson, "How Does Finland's Top-Ranking Education System Work?" accessed December 2, 2020, https://www.weforum.org/agenda/2019/02/how-does-finland-s-top-ranking-education-system-work.

52 Ibid.

53 V. Strauss, "Perspective—What Finland Is Really Doing to Improve Its Acclaimed Schools," August 30, 2019, accessed December 2, 2020, https://www.washingtonpost.com/education/2019/08/30/what-finland-is-really-doing-improve-its-acclaimed-schools/.

54 Ibid.

55 Ibid.

56 Ibid.

57 Ibid.

58 K. Dickinson, "Standardized Tests and Finland's Education System," May 21, 2019, accessed February 11, 2021, https://bigthink.com/politics-current-affairs/standardized-testing?rebelltitem=1#rebelltitem1.

59 W. Abby Jackson, "Finland Has One of the World's Best Education Systems. Here's How It Compares to the US," accessed December 2, 2020, https://www.weforum.org/agenda/2016/11/finland-has-one-of-the-worlds-best-education-systems-four-ways-it-beats-the-us.

60 Ibid.

61 Ibid.

62 "See the Average College Tuition in 2020–2021," accessed February 11, 2021, https://www.usnews.com/education/best-colleges/paying-for-college/articles/paying-for-college-infographic.

63 Abby Jackson, "Finland Has One of the World's Best Education Systems."

64 Hancock, "Why Are Finland's Schools Successful?"

65 Ibid.

66 C. Emma, "Finland's Low-Tech Take on Education," May 28, 2014, accessed December 3, 2020, https://www.politico.com/story/2014/05/finland-school-system-107137.

67 Ibid.

CHAPTER 5

Bullying in Schools

> All who rage against you will surely be ashamed and disgraced; those who oppose you will be as nothing and perish. Though you search for your enemies, you will not find them. Those who wage war against you will be as nothing at all. For I am the Lord, your God, who takes hold of your right hand and says to you. Do not fear; I will help you. (Isaiah 41:11–13 NIV)

One of the most concerning problems in American schools today is bullying. Cyberbullying is perhaps even bigger than in-person bullying, and that is addressed in another book. Currently our focus is solely on bullying occurring in person. It has become a problem that is growing at alarming rates. We have been given a reprieve from face-to-face bullying due to the pandemic and children learning from home. However, with the return of normalcy and the end of COVID-19, rest assured it will return to schools (especially in the United States), affecting students in every grade level.

We have all seen movies and television shows where children are bullied. I wish there were a simple answer to the problem. Bullying can be the culmination of many things. It is my belief that all children want to be loved and accepted, even bullies. In many cases, children who are bullies have chosen the wrong people with whom to be friends, or they are themselves victims of bullying, maybe even from a parent.

If you have a child who is or has been a victim of bullying, you know the feelings of helplessness and concern a parent may experience. Children do not want parents involved for fear of making the situation worse. Yet parents want to help and solve children's problems, especially those problems we feel are doing emotional damage.

Some victims have taken their own lives because of their sense of helplessness. This is why we need to be careful and always keep lines of communication open. When children are feeling this out of control, we need to be prepared to listen and get help. I hope this never happens in your family. Our aim is to equip schools and groups with the information to implement programs that have been used with positive results.

I like to think of it like insurance: we get it and hope we do not need it. If bullying is a problem at your child's school, recruit other parents, teachers, and administrators, as well as the community, to implement one of the programs discussed or another program you have researched.

As a word of warning, these schools are constantly being marketed to by companies promising outstanding results. Before you recommend a program, do the research. Also, find out what is currently being used and get feedback from the teachers and school personnel about why it is not working.

Just as every child is different, so is every situation of bullying. There are no one-size-fits-all solutions. But there are things we as parents and teachers can do. Parents and the PTA should form a committee to investigate the programs. Before recommending any program, take the time to contact a school using this particular program. Find out if it truly works, if there were hiccups getting it started, and if they are planning to make any changes to it.

Many parents believe bullying is a school problem, but it is also a home problem. Children who are not taught to respect others or who have difficulty handling uncomfortable situations may be more prone to becoming bullies. In many cases, bullying may reflect home life. An older brother or sister may be bullying a student, or Mom's boyfriend could be aggressive toward a child. There are any number of reasons a child is aggressive at school. And likewise, a bully could be a victim of bullying in earlier grades at school. At any rate, the problem should not be considered solely the problem of the school; it should be a problem of parents and school, working together.

In an effort to prevent bullying, some elementary schools have implemented programs such as Positive Behavior Intervention and Support (PBIS). PBIS is designed to reinforce good behavior with tickets as rewards, thereby discouraging bad behavior. I am familiar with this program because it was mandatory in the schools where I taught. In my last years of teaching, my workload was split between three elementary schools. I was able to participate and observe this program firsthand at different schools. I will not dispute any of the research found on the PBIS website. However, the PBIS model did not work in any of the schools to which I was assigned.

One of the biggest issues with PBIS is the interpretation of the program by the county and school administrators. At one school, children were rewarded simply for replying "Good morning" or speaking when addressed by an adult. A party was given at the end of each grading period for students displaying good behavior. One school administrator wanted all students to be able to attend the reward party. Children were quick to realize that good behavior was not rewarded if all students attended. Disrespectful and disruptive children were also rewarded. This led to the students' expectation (and even demand) of reward tickets, even when they were not earned. Students were being rewarded for doing things they should already be doing, such as being polite or putting away their coats and books before school. Students were not going above and beyond to earn rewards for displaying good character traits. They were doing less and expecting more.

This type of system attempts to bribe students to make good choices and display good character. This did not work at my schools and will not work in the long term with the current model. Tangible rewards do not reinforce good behavior or build character. Quite the opposite, when children expect to be rewarded for acts of kindness or for following the rules, they will become discouraged and may even stop the positive behavior when the world does not constantly reward them.

EXPECTATIONS

Instead of "buying" products, parents and teachers need to set minimum expectations of all children. There are certain things parents should be training their children from birth, and teachers should build on that. These include but are not limited to the following.

- Be respectful to everyone, even those with whom you disagree.
- Follow the rules wherever you are (home, school, bus, playground, etc.).
- Be kind to everyone, especially those without friends.
- Do not take anything that does not belong to you; if you borrow something, return it.
- Put away your things.
- Do not argue; disagreements are solved by listening to what others have to say.
- Accept punishment or correction for anything you have done wrong, even if you feel it is not deserved.

Unlike the current trends, these expectations do not make someone a weaker person. It takes a person with strong character and respect to accept punishment they do not think they deserve. Fighting and arguing about every perceived injustice creates more chaos, lack of trust, and insecurity. Yes, the world is not always fair, and sometimes we are judged wrongly. This is the way of the world.

The Bible teaches to expect times of hardships. Life is never promised to be easy. Christians are promised the glories in heaven, which is their true home. There are many times in the Bible when we are told life on earth will be difficult, but our rewards are in heaven. We should also be teaching this to our children.

For us to teach our children that life is always easy, it is always fair, and they will always be winners is not only going against the teachings in the Bible but is also setting them up for anxiety and even depression when life is difficult.

> But we also rejoice in our sufferings because we know that suffering produces perseverance; perseverance, character; and character, hope. And hope does not disappoint us, because God has poured out his love into our hearts by the Holy Spirit, whom he has given us. (Romans 5:3–5 NIV)

When these times come—and they will—we should be preparing our children for them and teaching them God is always with us and will never forsake us. I love Disney movies where the unfortunate and mistreated are later turned into beautiful, well-loved characters with a happy ending. Sometimes life is like the Disney movie, but more times it is not. It is our job as parents and teachers to prepare our children for the times when life is unfair.

I encourage prayer during these times, teaching children to take our burdens to God. Rather than making a cause on earth, take the time to teach the character of the followers of Jesus. There will be many wrongs done to our children; I have experienced these too.

> Be strong and courageous. Do not be afraid or terrified because of them, for the Lord your God goes with you; he will never leave you nor forsake you. (Deuteronomy 31:6 NIV)

Before taking the burden upon ourselves, we should seek first the kingdom of God and His will. Pray for guidance, and God will lead you during a difficult situation.

> Then Daniel said to the king, "O king, live forever! My God sent his angel and shut the lions' mouths, and they have not harmed me, because I was found blameless before him; and also before you, O king, I have done no harm." (Daniel 6:21–22 NIV)

COMMUNICATION

Children need to feel free to tell you when something happens. If a child has disobeyed you and finds himself in a bad situation, he needs to be able to come to you without fear. But if he cannot come to you, there needs to be another trusted adult he can turn to. If a child does not have an adult he can confide in, he will confide in a peer—and probably take bad advice that could make the situation much worse.

Take everything your child tells you seriously. If your child feels you do not believe him, then he will not bother trying to convince you. Instead of jumping to judgment, take a breath, stay calm, and ask questions. Learn as much as possible about what has happened.

Most times we will want to solve the problem for them. After all, they are our children, and we love them. This makes us feel better. The problem is handled, and that is the end. But it did not help our children. When we solve a problem for them, we are not showing them we have confidence in them to solve it themselves. And we are not giving them these valuable experiences to build on as life presents more difficult problems. Let them solve their own problems if it does not involve their emotional or physical health.

There are times children will not tell parents or other adults for fear of how their parents will react. Be aware this is a real possibility many times in their lives. When a situation is out of children's control, they need to have the assurance they can come to us for advice. No matter what the situation, do not overreact. This will lead children to fear you as well as the bully.

If the bullying goes as far as causing emotional and even physical harm, parents should intervene. Never place your children in a place of danger.

- Talk to your child and get as much information as possible. If your child is reluctant to tell everything, explain that you simply want to understand what has happened and what is going on.
- Never be too busy to listen to your child.

- Take a breath. Write down as much information as you can about what your child has revealed.
- Schedule an appointment with the teacher, principal, and guidance counselor. If necessary, keep your child out of school until you feel other adults are informed and a plan has been put in place to prevent a future occurrence.
- During the meeting, take your documentation, and document this meeting as well. Stress to the school personnel that you do not expect your child to have any negative consequences because of your meeting. I encourage you not to go into the meeting angry or blaming anyone. You need these people on your side.
- Because bullying is such a large problem in schools today, you may find the staff not as concerned as they should be. This is why you need to have the written account you recorded earlier.
- If the matter is resolved, be sure to send a note thanking those involved for their help.
- If the matter is not resolved, schedule another meeting through an email, copy the school superintendent and members of the school board, and invite them to the meeting. I encourage you to use this as a last resort, but if it is needed, by all means use it.
- Stay in touch with the people on your email list to update them on the situation. Thank them when resolved.

You must keep an open mind when your child is the victim of a bully. It is always better, especially for the victim, if the situation can be defused. If we constantly show our children the way to solve problems is by losing our temper or making demands of others, we are not teaching them how to find peaceful, calm ways to solve their own problems as adults. They are watching us and learning from our actions.

TWO ANTI-BULLYING PROGRAMS
WITH POSITIVE RESULTS

With all of this in mind, there are two programs that have found success in bully prevention. Keep in mind the one element needed to have a successful outcome is soliciting the entire school to get onboard. This may require parents recruiting other parents, teachers, and administrators, but never underestimate the power of parents to influence decisions. If parents find success with a program, the next step should be to present it to school board members. The school board ultimately decides which programs to implement.

Both of these programs recognize there are three types of people involved in bullying: the bully, the victim, and the bystander. The bully is the person inciting the hurtful remarks and actions. The process of bullying is defined as "Any unwanted aggressive behavior(s) by another youth or group of youths who are not siblings or current dating partners that involve an observed or perceived power imbalance and is repeated multiple times or is highly likely to be repeated."[29]

When talking with teachers and school administrators, they want to be sure parents understand what bullying is and is not. This is incredibly important for parents to understand, especially helicopter parents, because there are many instances where immature boys use insults or teasing as a way to flirt. Boys mature slower than girls, so they do not understand how to talk to girls and use teasing as a way to get attention. Keep in mind that once the girl asks the boy to stop, the boy needs to understand he must end the behavior. This is the point where harmless flirting starts to become bullying. The key is that the bully understands that the behavior is harmful. Intervention is crucial for both the bully and the target. Without assistance, the problem behavior persists with the negative outcomes increasing.

> Bullies are people who use conflict as a means for obtaining power. Some young people grow out of this; others don't and become old bullies.–
> —Bob Goff (McKee, p.80)[30]

As a final thought about bullies, please remember that some bullies are being bullied at home and so bully others to gain power. They are learning it because they are living it. Some bully because they think it makes them look powerful in front of their friends. There are any number of reasons people bully others, but none make it acceptable. Some even turn out to be adult bullies. Whatever the reason, we must prepare our children to be able to deal with them.

The victim is the target of the bullying. Some victims are chosen because they may seem weak or different, or they may appear to be loners. Whatever the reason, they are not at fault and should not be made to feel as if they have done something wrong or have encouraged bullying. Victims need most of all to be heard. It is vital that they feel they can talk to an adult. Children should not feel there is no way to escape this, or that it will never end. Keep communication lines open with your children. If victims do not feel comfortable talking to parents, they need another adult to be able to confide in.

In desperate situations, victims have taken their own lives. We do not want to see this happen ever again. Whatever victims are feeling, they must be assured there is someone who understands how they feel.

Generally, face-to-face bullying occurs in front of a group of people. This provides the bully with support and encouragement and makes him or her feel like a leader in a group. Bystanders are now being considered the people with the most power to change the situation.

Do not wait until your child is a victim to talk to them about bullying. Encourage them to support the victim, to avoid giving the bully the kind of attention they want. Talk to children about the important role a bystander has in helping prevent others from being bullied. The hope is that if the bully does not receive encouragement and is in fact, ignored, this will remove the incentive to bully others.

Intervention with bystanders involves role play exercises and models of how to speak to a bully. It also involves creating a culture of empathy.

> And these words that I command you today shall be
> on your heart. You shall teach them diligently to your
> children and shall talk of them when you sit in your

house, and when you walk by the way, and when you lie down, and when you rise. (Deuteronomy 6:6–7 NIV)

AGAIN, LET US TAKE A LOOK AT FINLAND

In Finland's educational system, the administration uses a program called KiVa, meaning "against bullying." Its focus on prevention, intervention, and monitoring is key to their success. "Universal actions are taught to every student through a series of lessons and online games designed to prevent bullying. Indicated actions are used to intervene and diffuse a bullying incident once it has occurred."[31] In simple terms, the KiVa program educates children through lessons about bullying and how to react. It also teaches children what to do if they are bystanders.

> One of the most important aspects of KiVa is engaging bystanders. The students are taught empathy through the different games and simulations. In the various scenarios they are given, they must choose what actions they will take what consequences might come of those actions. Students are also given support and feedback on how to approach victims of bullying and make sure they are okay. The games allow students to "practice" being nice and thinking through what to say to someone who is feeling excluded or unwelcome in a group. This improves the students' abilities to be empathetic and supportive to victims.

> Being more supportive and empathetic of the victims also dis-incentivizes the bully to act again. Most children that bully others do so to gain status, exert power, or get attention. Putting the focus and attention on the victim is unrewarding to the bully and creates a culture where bullying is socially unacceptable.[32]

Schools in Finland began using this program in the early 2000s and saw positive results almost immediately. There has been a reluctance for the United States to follow suit, claiming the diversity of US students as a reason.[33] Whatever the reason, it is a better method of dealing with bullying than programs I have observed in my many years spent in public education.

Students in the United States have developed the "me first" agenda, focusing on themselves and "what's in it for me." There are exceptions, but even these students are unprepared and unequipped with what to do when seeing someone being bullied. The focus to empower and direct bystanders with ways to "make a difference" and become a "hero" to a victim is the missing piece of the solution we are all seeking. Empathy, the ability of putting oneself in the shoes of the victim, should become a part of the curriculum in every school. This is not just a means for dealing with bullying; it is the way Jesus teaches by example, and it is the way we are instructed in the Bible. We should be showing empathy for our fellow man each day, demonstrated by the way we live and the example we set for our family.

> When he saw the crowds, he had compassion on them, because they were harassed and helpless, like sheep without a shepherd. (Matthew 9:36 NIV)

> Carry each other's burdens, and in this way, you will fulfill the law of Christ. (Galatians 6:2 NIV)

ANOTHER PROGRAM WORTH OUR TIME

Point Break is an anti-bullying and intervention one-day workshop. It focuses on: "bullying, teasing, reaching for help, judging others, improving a hopeful outlook, ability to openly express oneself, and having empathy for others."[34] This program is designed for high school students. Point Break recognizes that the high school years are a time when students feel most vulnerable. Thoughts of suicide, and even suicide itself, occurs at alarming numbers. In this program, students spend the day in groups, some small and others large, all with the goal to recognize they are not alone in the way they feel or what they are going through in life.

They go through a series of activities and discussions to allow students to see and hear others who share the same experiences. The aim is for them to realize they are not alone and are valued. At the end of the day, students participate in an activity called Cross the Line, where students cross the line on the floor if they have experienced the scenario described by the leader. In this whole-group activity, students can visibly see they have friends and classmates who are going through the same ordeals as they are[6]. Please check out this program online; there are YouTube clips describing it. This program is especially important for young people going through a difficult situation that they feel they have no control over. This may include the divorce of parents, a breakup with a boyfriend or girlfriend, varied health problems, the death of a family member, being bullied, or any number of insecurities.

MORE SUGGESTIONS IF YOUR CHILD IS BEING BULLIED

Children need a trusting relationship with parents where they feel comfortable confiding in them. Try to be that person. Respect their concerns and above all listen. We are too quick to add our advice before we have fully heard the problem. Parents become so busy that we only want to get beyond this obstacle and move on to the next task. Whenever our children feel secure enough to confide in us, we must not take it lightly. What is important to them needs to be important to us.

Jonathan McKee, in his book *The Bullying Breakthrough Real Help for Parents and Teachers of the Bullied, Bystanders, and Bullies*, gives ten things parents can do if their children are being bullied. McKee gives us a firsthand account of his life being bullied. He also describes how he and his wife handled the situation when their own son was a victim of bullying. Just as no two children are alike, there are no two situations alike. You may find some of his suggestions helpful, and others are not as helpful. But the best part of his list is it comes from his own sense of helplessness as a child being bullied.

1. Do Not Overreact!

    - Overreaction never helps. It can increase your child's anxiety.
    - Avoid minimizing the problem. Do not simply ignore it.
    - Do not rush to blame. Never ask, "Well, what did you do to provoke him?"
    - Resist immediately trying to fix the problem by saying, "Just do this …" Remember, if they are telling you, they need to talk.
    - Avoid meddling when your child does not want your help: "We're going to go talk with those bullies' parents right now!" This can keep your child from telling you about any future issues.
    - This is one of the most difficult disciplines for parents. Instead of rushing down to the school to talk with the principal and "fix it," start with empathy. Talk to your child about how he or she is feeling. Validate those feelings by listening. Instead of taking over the conversation by offering your experiences and outcomes, ask if your child wants to tell you more. You can also ask your child if he or she would like your help in finding a solution. If your child is being bullied about clothing or physical appearance (and he or she wants it), you can offer to help change it. Try to find creative ways to be of assistance instead of solving the problem. This allows your child's character to grow and encourages problem-solving skills. Of course, if this problem is intense with personality changes, it is time to involve a professional.

2. Step into Their World

- Almost every story has one common denominator: an adult who did not take time to understand.
- Have empathy. Step into your kid's shoes and walk around in what they are experiencing. Life for kids today is so much different than it was for you. Instead of overreacting and making them feel worse about an already embarrassing situation, slow down, watch, and listen. Then say, "I'm so glad you told me."

3. Seek Settings Where They Open Up

- Seek places and times where your child feels safe talking to you, maybe at bedtime.
- Enter their world. Really think about your child's experience. How would you feel if you were him or her? Tell your child you do not understand if the experience is difficult.
- Young people love being the expert. Allow them to show you the ropes of a world you do not know about. If they feel your interest and empathy, more talking is encouraged.

4. Be Proactive about Building Identity

- Bullying is an attack a child's self-esteem. The roots of self-esteem sink deep into the question, "Who am I?"
- Bullying can actually create PTSD-like symptoms. Common signs are feelings of worthlessness and helplessness, both of which feed anxiety.
- Every child is good at something. It is our job to discover what it is and encourage it.
- Affirm children in their identity in Christ.
- Confident children know who they are and how they will present themselves to the world. Helping our children develop identity helps them develop comfort with themselves.

- People with a strong sense of self are less targeted.
- Connection is a huge part of the equation. Seek out opportunities for children to socialize while doing activities they enjoy, increasing the opportunities for them to meet someone with similar interests.
- Do not simply drop off children at karate or baseball practice. This might be dropping them into a den of lions. Watch children the first time, without being noticed. Be careful, though, or they could be labeled a "mama's boy." Social connection is extremely therapeutic for all children.

5. Give Them a Chance to Serve, and Remember to Lead by Example

- Another way to help hurting kids feel valued is to give them the opportunity to help others. Take children to the local food shelter to cook, clean, and serve food to the homeless. This experience can be life-changing for many kids.
- Do you know a great remedy for depression? Do something to help others.
- Help the elderly with some yard work or housecleaning. These can be neighbors, relatives, or church members. Teach your children ways to give back to the community through service for needy people.

6. Build Confidence and Connection

- Find a place where they can eventually be an expert. Give them a chance to use their skills to assist others.
- Find activities that make them feel more self-assured socially. Remember that bullied kids tend to remove themselves socially, which triggers a downward spiral toward isolation. Getting involved in activities where they experience successful social encounters can help them develop basic social skills.

7. Dodge Danger Zones

If your child is not athletic, do not take them to sports camp. Be careful to not become a helicopter parent.

8. Teach Good Social Skills

- Teach them social skills, problem-solving, conflict management, and assertiveness. These are skills all kids need to know!
- Teach your children listening skills and how to ask questions; model this for them at early ages.
- Problem-solving and conflict management are skills most young people are lacking today. It seems we are developing a generation of kids who hide under headphones, blaring music while playing video games that encourage some to literally gun down anyone who disrespects them. We need to teach this generation how to solve conflict through social interaction. It is essential that parents talk with their children from early ages to model social behavior.

9. Teach Forgiveness

- Bullying is a unique kind of hurt.
- There is only one cure for the pain and bitterness: forgiveness.
- Read stories like the parable of the unmerciful servant in the Bible (Matthew 18:21–35).
- Give it to God: "God, I can't do it on my own. I need Your strength to forgive."

10. Get Support Yourself

If you are dealing with a kid who is hurting, reach out to others for prayer and emotional support. Do not hesitate to surround yourself with community in tough times like this. (McKee, pp.127-39)[35] There is a lot to learn from parents who have been through this.

The Lord's Prayer
Our Father, which art in heaven,
Hallowed be Thy name.
Thy kingdom come.
Thy will be done on earth, as it is in heaven.
Give us this day our daily bread.
And forgive us our trespasses,
as we forgive those that trespass against us.
And lead us not into temptation,
but deliver us from evil.
For Thine is the kingdom, the power, and the glory,
For ever and ever.
Amen.

TAKEAWAYS

- Prayer should be center of any bullying situation.
- There are usually three types of people when bullying occurs: the bully, the victim, and the bystander.
- Keep communication open with your children. Never make them think their problems are not important.
- Parents of victims should remain calm and get all the information possible before acting.
- Parents should allow children to handle situations, unless you feel they are in danger of emotional or physical harm.
- Have discussions about other situations of bullying they have observed or know about. Talk about how each person must have felt and the outcome.
- Investigate the KiVa program and Point Break. Talk to other parents and administrators about these programs.

CLOSING PRAYER

Everlasting Father,

As we complete our study, we humbly ask for Your blessing upon us and our children. Open our minds so that we are accepting and ready for Christian advice and opinions that will lead us to follow the path You have laid before us as Christian parents. Guide us, please, Lord, so that the words we speak to our children and the actions we take with them are pleasing to You. Allow us to be models of our Christian faith, foundations for Christian values and teachings in our families, and lights for our children to follow. Protect us, our Savior, from the evils of this world. Help us to recognize them so that we may protect our children. Lead us with the words to speak to prepare our children for these evils when they are not with us. Precious Lord, we ask Your blessing upon the adults who will help us to rear our children. Please instill knowledge, energy, and light in them so that they may be guides along our children's paths to You. We thank You this day for the many blessings that You have bestowed upon us and our families, especially those we do not recognize. God, we thank You for this opportunity to learn, grow, and share our time, ideas, and concerns with each other. We humbly ask that You lead us to be the best Christian parents we can be. In Jesus's name, we pray and praise.
Amen.

REFERENCES FOR CHAPTER 5

68 J. R. McKee, *The Bullying Breakthrough: Real Help for Parents and Teachers of the Bullied, Bystanders, and the Bullies* (Uhrichsville, OH: Shiloh Run, 2018).

69 Ibid.

70 K. Schreiber, "Finland Has an Efficient Way to Fight Bullying. Here's How," July 23, 2019, accessed December 7, 2020, https://www.buzzworthy.com/finland-way-to-fight-bullying/.

71 Ibid.

72 "Point Break for Schools—Build Empathy, Stop Bullying," December 13, 2013, accessed December 8, 2020, https://www.youtube.com/watch?v=X0PQUefyFQA.

73 McKee, *The Bullying Breakthrough*.

CHAPTER QUESTIONS

Chapter 1: American Students Are Tested so Much

Questions Prior to Reading

1. What are your thoughts about the standardized testing given to students in many public schools?
2. Describe the purpose of Common Core and testing as you understand it.
3. Describe the differences in the way your children learn today and the way you were taught. Do you think today's educational system is better or worse? Explain your thinking.
4. Take time to ponder, then discuss the top two of three things you want your children to gain from education. Then explain why these are important to you.
5. Who do you believe is responsible for educating your children?

Questions After the Study

1. Do you think the amount of testing required by students is necessary? Explain. Have you changed your opinion about testing?
2. Reflect on your feelings about the number of companies profiting from students constant testing.
3. As you read about the underprivileged children, how did you feel about their perspective? Can you put yourself in their shoes and how difficult it must be for them? Do you as a Christian feel an obligation to these children?

4. Do you think we should be concerned about these test scores and brag when our children score at the top? Do you think this is pleasing to God? What do you think is pleasing to God?

5. What is our responsibility as parents to the education of our children? How hard is it for us to go against the current trends in education? What obstacles would need to be overcome to make changes?

Chapter 2: The Internet and Our Brains

Questions Prior to Reading

1. How do you think the Internet and computer devices impact our brains and the brains of our children?

2. Do you think Satan uses our weaknesses, such as our love of the Internet, to deceive us? Explain.

3. How do you feel about children getting behind if they are not constantly connected to technology?

4. Why do you think most people are so anxious do give their children computers, iPads, or Chromebooks?

5. What is your philosophy of education? What do think its purpose is for your children?

Questions After the Study

1. Reflect on your thoughts about the effects to the brain and our ability to reason with technology.

2. What are your thoughts about parents giving infants and toddlers iPads and devices to distract and occupy them? What do you think are the long-term effects of this?

3. Do you think some parents are allowing devices to read to children as a substitution for human interaction? What do you think is the impact of this?

4. What kind of life do you think technology is preparing children for? Do you think they will become more isolated from the world as they become more tech driven?
5. Are you concerned the executives of Silicon Valley are choosing low-tech for their own children? Do they know more than most people?

Chapter 3: Computers, Devices, and Our Children

Questions Prior to Reading

1. Name some things you feel are appropriate for adults, but not for children. How do we determine what is not appropriate for children?
2. Describe something you have seen other parents allow children to do that you feel is inappropriate.
3. What are your thoughts about social media and parents who post about their children?
4. If money was no object, describe the ideal school and classroom for your child.
5. Briefly describe your own attachment to technology and social media.

Questions After the Study

1. Do you think technology has caused problems within families and for children? If so, what?
2. Review the comments of Mr. Rogers. How do his remarks compare to your style of raising children?
3. What are your thoughts and reactions to the executives of Silicon Valley and their philosophy of educating their children?
4. Describe the effects you would anticipate at your home if you used technology only for required school and work. Be sure to include the effects on the adults as well as the children.
5. Is technology rushing children to grow up too fast? Explain.

Chapter 4: American Schools Are Doing It Wrong

Questions Prior to Reading

1. What are your thoughts about the American education system compared to other countries?
2. Why do you think America is beginning to fall behind other countries in education?
3. Discuss things you think can be done to improve education.
4. Take a few minutes to compare your experience as a student with today's student experience. Specifically discuss those things which are worse today and the reasons why they could be worse.
5. Name two or three ways you think American education can be improved.

Questions After the Study

1. After reading and discussing the material, do you think one education system is better than the other? Explain.
2. How important do you think standardized test scores should be in evaluating performance? Do you think there should be changes made in this system of evaluation?
3. What are your thoughts about the education system in Finland?
4. How do you think the United States' educational system is measuring up to the Bible, understanding these are public schools?
5. Has the competitive spirit of Americans influenced the way we teach? Explain.

Chapter 5: Bullying in Schools

Questions Prior to Reading

1. How much of a problem do you think bullying in schools is?
2. Have you considered how you would handle this situation if it happened to your children? Explain.

3. Do you think the Bible gives us instructions about bullying? What do you think it advises?

4. Some children have considered suicide when they feel trapped in a situation where they are being bullied. How do you think these situations can be prevented?

5. Do you think there are times children are teasing each other that is not really bullying? How can children tell the difference?

CHAPTER ENDNOTES

1   Bakan, J. (2011). *Childhood under siege: How big business ruthlessly targets children*. New York, NY: Free press.

2   Ibid

3   Ibid

4   Miner, B., & Barbara Miner (barbaraminer@ameritech.net) is a freelance writer and former managing editor of Rethinking Schools. (2020, October 22). Testing Companies Mine for Gold. Retrieved November 05, 2020, from https://rethinkingschools.org/articles/keeping-public-schools-public-testing-companies-mine-for-gold/

5   Ibid

6   Ibid

7   Ibid

8   Strauss, V. (2019, April 24). Everything you need to know about Common Core - Ravitch. Retrieved November 06, 2020, from https://www.washingtonpost.com/news/answer-sheet/wp/2014/01/18/everything-you-need-to-know-about-common-core-ravitch/

9   Ibid

10 Bakan, J. (2011). *Childhood under siege: How big business ruthlessly targets children*. New York, NY: Free press.

11 Strauss, V. (2019, April 24). Everything you need to know about Common Core - Ravitch. Retrieved November 06, 2020, from https://www.washingtonpost.com/news/answer-sheet/wp/2014/01/18/everything-you-need-to-know-about-common-core-ravitch/

12 Kardaras, N. (2016). *Glow kids*. New York, NY: St. Martin's.

13 Ibid

14 Ibid

15 Ibid

16 Ibid

17 Ibid

18 Goyal, N. (2016, April 06). These Politicians Think Your Kids Need High-Stakes Testing-but Not Theirs. Retrieved November 18, 2020, from https://www.thenation.com/article/archive/these-politicians-think-your-kids-need-high-stakes-testing-but-not-theirs/

19 Ibid

20 FAQs About Waldorf. (n.d.). Retrieved November 19, 2020, from https://www.waldorfeducation.org/waldorf-education/faqs-about-waldorf

21 Ibid

22 Carr, N. G. (2010). *The shallows: How the internet is changing the way we think, read and remember = The shallows: What the Internet is doing to our brains.* London: Atlantic Books.

23 Ibid

24 Ibid

25 Riley, N>S> (2018). Be the parent, please. United States, PA: Templeton Press.

26 Ibid

27 Ibid

28 Carr, N. G. (2010). *The shallows: How the internet is changing the way we think, read and remember - The shallows: What the Internet is doing to our brains.* London: Atlantic Books.

29 McKee, J. R. (2018). *The bullying breakthrough: Real help for parents and teachers of the bullied, bystanders, and the bullies.* Uhrichsville, OH: Shiloh Run Press, an imprint of Barbour Publishing.

30 Ibid

31 Schreiber, K. (2019, July 23). Finland Has an Efficient Way to Fight Bullying. Here's How. Retrieved December 07, 2020, from https://www.buzzworthy.com/finland-way-to-fight-bullying/

32 Ibid

33 Biddletube01. (2013, December 13). Point Break for Schools - Build Empathy, Stop Bullying. Retrieved December 08, 2020, from https://www.youtube.com/watch?v=X0PQUefyFQA

34 Ibid

35 McKee, J. R. (2018). *The bullying breakthrough: Real help for parents and teachers of the bullied, bystanders, and the bullies.* Uhrichsville, OH: Shiloh Run Press, an imprint of Barbour Publishing.

ABOUT THE AUTHOR

Sylvia McCrory taught eighteen years in public schools, has taught Sunday school and led Bible studies and is dedicated to following God. Married, she is a Christian mom to three grown children. McCrory lives near Wilmington, North Carolina. Visit her online at https:// christianparentingtoday.org.

Melissa Wingfield, a retired public-school teacher with twenty-seven years of service, is a church elder and is a dedicated church leader. Married, she lives near Greensboro, North Carolina, and is the Christian mother of two adult children.

Printed in the United States
by Baker & Taylor Publisher Services